A Woman's Journey
(Part One)

A Guide to Overcome Real Life Obstacles

BY: ERICA NICOLE

**LIVE LIFE,
DON'T LET LIFE LIVE YOU.**

A Woman's Journey
Copyright © 2023 by Erica Nicole Jackson

All rights reserved. No part of this publication may be reproduced, stored in a retrieval system, or transmitted in any form or by any means- electronic, mechanical, photocopy, recording, or any other manner- without written permission of the publisher except for the use of brief quotations in printed reviews.

Requests for information should be addressed to:
Erica Nicole Jackson
enjackson4@icloud.com

ISBN 978-1-7346599-4-8 (print)
　　　978-1-7346599-5-5 (ebook)

All rights reserved.

Cover design: Virgil Odell
Interior design: Mony
Editor: Dr. Tamika S. Hood
Printed in the United States of America

Contents

DEDICATION 1
PREFACE 2
INTRODUCTION 7
CHAPTER ONE
    EARLY DAYS 8
CHAPTER TWO
    DISTRACTIONS 14
CHAPTER THREE
    FEAR OF THE UNKNOWN 33
CHAPTER FOUR
    ACCEPTANCE 52
EPILOGUE 73

DEDICATION

To all the people who have lived truly,
over and beyond the edginess of reality.
To my entire family who have watched me grow
−to my greatest supporters: My Mother and my Father; Dot- Dot (My grandmother)
Kendra and Amore (my dear sisters),
my niece Khylei-Jae,
all of my aunts and uncles,
all of my friends,
and all who have taught me all that I know.
To my husband, Jason;
Sweet baby girl Ayden, my little bodyguards Jason Jr., Lenox and Hero,
I love you with all my heart.

PREFACE

While writing the first draft of this book in my notes sometime in 2015, I just knew that I had a story –or a message to pass along. At the time, I was so fixated on the message. Maybe this story was one I wasn't so ready to tell at the time, and certainly, in the space of time, days, hours, weeks, months, and years of growth between then and now, I have a fuller story to tell. And this story is surely one that's been in the making.

If my memory –and my rough jottings turned drafts– serve me well, the only certainty about what I was doing back then was that I wanted this book to be in chapters. I wasn't even sure how the structure would play out when I finally started to put my experiences into words. Well… I wanted this to be about my life. Then again, I wanted this to be about the things that I have accomplished, how I've tackled things that we face as mothers, wives, entrepreneurs, women, and so on.

We all have different ways in which we cope with life and its variants of challenges. Munching on these stories, experiences, and lessons was a coping mechanism for me. I just wanted to pour the feelings out on paper, to tell the papers –that I've grown accustomed to its flipping sound– how I felt about life generally. When I return to add flesh to these writings, I find that some of these things still are true even though I have grown from the person I was six years ago. Only, this time around, those drafts would come to include stories, experiences, and examples of simple things that we go through each day.

To be able to do justice to this process, I first have to say a big thank you in what should be a dedication to everyone that I'll be mentioning in the Dedication. They have all played major roles in my life. To become who I am today took their stories and experiences combined.

First, I will dedicate this book to all the strong women and men who have gone through many trials and tribulations in their life, and who are working to be the best that they can be and doing their best. There is never a person around sometimes to tell you to keep up the good work or to keep you motivated. I want this book to be a reminder that we all go through things, and we can get through them if we focus on what is our purpose. I want to be able to reach out to people and let them know that it's okay to go through things, and I want this book to motivate individuals to let them know it is not always what it looks like on the outside. We all are humans, and we go through things.

I also want to dedicate this book to my family. I love my family first because everyone here is unique. I always say that my family is my life, and that pretty much sums it up. It doesn't matter what we're doing on a day-to-day basis or where we all go, we always find ways to keep in touch with each other. If I call anyone when in trouble and need them, they'll be on the way without even knowing what was going on. That's what I call a family: very loyal and committed. My cousin, **Elyse**, we pretty much grew up together as sisters. I stayed over at her house every other weekend when I could. We had our routine, we enjoyed picking up Chinese food from the mall on Fridays and going to get a new pair of jeans. We then would walk around the neighborhood on Saturdays and just enjoy outside amid laughs and stories that we shared about our classmates. I also appreciate all my aunts and uncles who have been there for me. You would think I had four or five moms and dads because there's not one person who's never there when you call. Everyone sets huge examples of what it means to be strong women and men. They each are loving and committed to their family. There is never a day that goes by that I don't think of something they told me or a situation in which they've helped me through.

I also dedicate this book to my **mom**. My mom is one very tough woman who doesn't let too much off. Instead, she puts on a tough image and hard shell. Although there have been times that I needed that affection, that tough outlook has, however, made it easy for me to focus on things in my life, and to be more capable of separating my feelings from business. This has helped in my success. She has always worked hard and given us everything and anything that we needed. I can say that we were never lacking the basic things while growing up because of her. She has always gone above and made sure we were happy regardless of whatever was going on in our lives. Her commitment was to make sure we enjoyed life.

To my **dad**, even though we're so much alike and bump heads, his famous saying, "gotta work your plan, plan your work," has helped me be the individual I am today. It has helped mold me into a leader, one capable of tackling things others would have thought daunting while making sure I provide, defend, and protect my family. He has always treated my sisters and me like the most special people in the world. Regardless of where he was, his kind and motivational words still made us feel protected and loved as if he was right there with us. In my darkest moments, I got through them knowing that if I couldn't figure out a way, he would be there.

I also want to dedicate this book to my husband, **Jason**. He is my biggest fan and supporter. In his own way, he lets me know I am special and that I have the capability to tackle anything. He often does not know how to show it, but his allowing me to be me and act impulsively and do what makes me happy, even if it is over the top, is what makes us have such a true bond. He never placed a limit on what I needed for me to be happy. Although he takes drastic risks –even ones that I'm not so comfortable with, they are ones that show he is willing to do whatever is needed to ensure my happiness and my children's security. This has helped make me stronger, even enough to write this book. I would never have imagined being as vulnerable as I am today. He reminds me at every turn that I am human and that it is okay to say so when I need something. He lets me know that I don't have to put on a face each day and that it's okay to let others know that you need their support. I am indeed grateful for what we have built as a family and the courageous drive that we both have to provide a legacy for our family.

I would like to dedicate this book to my dear sisters, **Kendra** and **Amore**. Amore is my youngest sister. She has autism. Although she has autism, she is still very confident and happy. Her smile makes you smile regardless of what you have going on. Her giving me a kiss when she sees me makes my day, letting me know that she knows "her big sister is here." My sister **Kendra**…my ride or die, words cannot express how I feel about her. I can't hold back the tears that come to my eyes as I write this, thinking how much I appreciate her and am so proud of her. She is a great mother, sister, aunt, and wife, among the many more roles she plays. She is there whenever I need her. Even though we have busy lives, we still make time to ensure each other is okay. We ensure we meet up to see each other. This is key for me, we don't rely on just a phone, we put effort into *presence*. Being in each other's presence brings a sense of calmness and peace to me. There are no better words to express how I feel about you two beyond "I love you, and I am so proud of who you have become."

To my niece, **Khylei-Jae**, you hold a special place in my heart. She is so skilled and artistic. I can't wait to see your work framed in museums and shops when you get older.

To my grandmother, **Dorothy Lee**, for whom words can't express her love. She finds a way to let you know that you are missed or that you are special when she is not around. In my darkest moments, when I was unsure of myself, her kind words helped motivate me to keep going. They have also helped me to make tough decisions in my life. She has set a great example of how to be genuine and be the best person you can be always. She sets the bar high and continues to raise it as she sets an example and touches all that she encounters.

Also, I would like to dedicate this book to my best friends from the **Achievable Dream Black Group**, whom we have been through some things that no one would ever know. We still repeat those same banners we recited when we were younger in the Achievable Dream gym. Thank you for always being there. And yea, when we get together, there is never a dull moment. We have established a bond that goes beyond measure. We don't have to talk every day, but there is an instant connection and an overwhelming amount of skill and experience that we each bring to the table when we hang out. **Jamie**, one of my best friends, has helped me to be strong through my toughest times. She was the only one who knew the struggles that I went through and was there every step of the way, even if I had to call her every hour. I will be forever thankful.

I would also like to dedicate this book to my amazing children, with whom I'm trying to leave a legacy. I have four children, each of whom holds a special place in my heart. First, there is my amazing, sweet, smart, beautiful, caring, and impressive baby girl, **Ayden**. She is my only girl and oldest child. I wouldn't trade the little dates that we go on together; the times when she sneaks in to sleep beside me; the times we watch a movie – just us girls; or the times when we share conversations on how to be her own person. My mission remains to ensure that I provide the tools and confidence she needs to tackle anything. Then there is **Jason Jr** –my twin– who is such an independent person who attracts people all over. His energy remains so contagious that I know it will take him far in life. There is also **Lenox,** with a creative mind, who often teaches even me through his kind gestures. My youngest son, **Baby Hero,** has eyes and a smile that lightens every room. I am trying to leave a legacy so my kids can do all they want and take their time being their own person in this tough world. Although I can get a little hard on them in my attempt to make them know the essence of hard work, it's so they can enjoy their lives without limits.

Sometimes, I think a little too hard that I'm not being able to enjoy life. But I want my kids not to have to feel that way. I love them with all my heart, and I just want them to be able to know that I am here whenever they need me; that I am never too busy for them.

I consider myself to be very driven, but I keep a lot of things to myself. This book is one I want to be able to show and speak about the things that I don't usually say. There are things that have happened in my life that people would not naturally know that I've been through. Many just see me as a calm, cool or relaxed individual –all of which I am– yet I've had some struggles. I also want to provide an expose into questions about how to portray each role and do it successfully. While I enjoy each role that I play and genuinely put my all into each role, making time for different people and things is always going to be a work in progress. I have trained myself to be patient when needed to fulfill what's needed; to give attention to each role I play; to enjoy helping others and making others happy while using this as motivation to enhance myself and better myself as a whole.

INTRODUCTION

This and more are what I want this book to show people, especially women and mothers who are like me or might be in similar situations, to find solace. I want to be able to fill in their gaps through my experiences and to be able to offer my advice also as an experienced mental health professional. You will laugh and cry as you turn the pages of this book meant to let readers know never to be ashamed of your true feelings and never to judge yourself. I want to help the reader realize that experiences and struggles such as those which we go through are merely phases. I want you to know that it's all up to us not to let life and all its uncertainties take over the wheel of our lives.

CHAPTER ONE
EARLY DAYS

I am a wife and business owner of over ten years; I am a sister, an aunt, a cousin, a friend, a niece, a daughter, a granddaughter, and a mother of four. I have multiple roles to play each day, and each is one I take very seriously.

B ut really…Who Am I?
I wish I knew.

Only my experiences and thoughts —whether good or bad— know who I truly am. I know that my abilities are excessive, thriving, mind-blowing, and eager to be the impossible. Yet, as a confident, successful, and exceptional individual on the outside, I am not so comfortable with life. Life is scary. It has, so many times in the past, spiraled beyond my control in unpredictable loops. While I can claim to be tough and always fighting the unknown with my guard up, I find myself surpassing happiness due to a lingering lack of confidence in my trust in others.

Will others be there for me as I would for them?

Do they mean what they say, and are their actions matching their words?

Most of the time, it doesn't. People are so moment-driven that they forget their foundation. This is one of my major fears when it comes to life and love. Moment-driven actions alter trust. At these moments, the norm is rejected or pushed to the darkest of corners in our subjective minds.

I wasn't always this complex. I can't say that I wasn't also driven or influenced by a life-altering moment.

I was born on Thanksgiving, a blessing strolling in with just 34 days left before 1987 takes the front seat. On the 27th of November 1986 in Newport News, a dynamic city in Virginia, I was welcomed with the Turkey stuffing as the first of three daughters. That's how I'd probably define it. Thanksgiving in Newport News was very sporadic. I used to go to my grandfather's house in Portsmouth or my great-aunts' house in Carrollton. We traveled to visit family members in the area on Thanksgiving. We always dressed up, so we planned our outfits and saved the best for Thanksgiving Day. At the time I was born, Thanksgiving to my mom was that time of the year when the community became the most glaring element of living in Newport News.

My parents were not married but were in a committed relationship. I have a huge family on both sides. My mom and father's side were very supportive growing up and are still very close to me. Whenever plans are in motion for the Annual Celebration in Lights, an animated display of over a million individual lights strewn together to mark the coming of the holidays, I remember my childhood and growing up.

Growing up in downtown Newport News, things were very laid back, yet you had to be very tough and aware. Although I was able to make my own decisions, I learned a lot from my neighbors, and I looked to them as family. We hung out together and walked to the neighborhood store every morning before school. We saw walking to the store as a luxury, giving us the thrill of independence. Neighbors also looked out for each other. We were told it wasn't safe to be out late at night, and family members who often stayed around the neighborhood or friends of parents took us to school when needed. We rotated who took us to school due to my mom's work schedule and there being an overflow of bus stops.

In our neighborhood, everyone knew each other. Everyone knew us because my sisters and I were close growing up. Our mom was also friendly and talked to everyone. Everyone often admired how my family took care of my youngest sister, who had autism. She was always well-

A Woman's Journey

dressed and taken care of, like Kendra, and I were, even though she could not voice her opinion on clothes and shoes.

A tradition that I'm so glad that we continued until we became older with my family was the trip to Disney World. Every other summer, my family would have trips, and my aunt would organize how we would get a charter bus to go as a family all together. Although it is over 700 miles away, it is one of the most memorable family vacations I can recall growing up. Disney world was so special because of the games we played on the buses, the laughs and jokes played with one another, and just the sense of togetherness that we all had, knowing that we always had someone to hang with. Even though I was not able to partake in all the activities, it remains one of the best vacations I had in my childhood.

My dad has always said, now and then, to "plan your work, work your plan." Back then, I'd tell him to stop saying that, but I actually live by this quote when I look back. From that saying, I think I got to place myself on some form of "how to live" guide, even as a child. I struggled, however. On most occasions, I'd be found trying to balance the responsibilities at home while being a child. This grossly affected how I related to my peers at school. They didn't have as many responsibilities as I had back then. I wasn't always at all the events that my friends were. I mostly had to leave house parties and events at 10 p.m. because my mom had to work. On most days, I would have to make sure that I was home so my mom and dad would know where I was when my mother went to school in case my dad had to leave for work. We had a very tight schedule, and I had to fill any space needed to ensure everyone's safety while my parents provided for us.

While having a very structured home environment, I did not have much time to engage in social activities outside of my family until I joined An Achievable Dream Academy (AADA). That program helped to introduce so many of us students to new experiences that helped to mold us into our current future. We all wore uniforms from 3rd to 8th grade, and I was only around a selected group of students from my class. As kids who did practically everything together, we became a family. I refer to everyone from the Academy as brothers and sisters today. We grew with each other and are still close to this day.

From the Academy, I got the earliest of my school memories and started to have a defined way of thinking from the lessons I was taught. From those early lessons, apart from mom's responsibilities and day-to-day planning, I learned always to try my best and never to say I can't. "Can't is not in your vocabulary" was always on one board or the other on the school's premises. There, I learned that if I always have good intentions, my effort will be seen in all I do.

From AADA, we proceeded to high school together at Heritage High School. I remember vividly the joy of wearing regular clothes for the first time in a school setting since 3rd grade. High school was a different experience altogether. I was involved in track, soccer, and varsity cheer leading. I also was in the National Honor Society.

I was a very introverted individual who did not show many emotions at all. I suppressed my feelings and focused on the tasks at hand, even as a child. This is something that, as an adult, I am not accustomed to doing, it has caused me to be successful in my career, yet it also hinders me because when my character is questioned, I become defensive. This is because I've always enjoyed protecting people and making sure things are going well. However, when I must go out of character, then I have a hard time adjusting, which has caused me to hold back from some of my biggest dreams. Although this suppression was some of my biggest setbacks, it also helped me to thrive as a child by engaging in events such as the Science Fair and Orchestra. These were very hands-on and social activities, which helped me show my confidence in front of others and define my personality.

After being involved in science and math a lot, I dream of different professions. While making decisions and trying to establish who I was, a dear family member of mine, my Aunt Victoria, passed away. She battled cancer and other illnesses, which prompted me to want to pursue medicine, and I entered college with a major in Pre-Med.

I attended Virginia Commonwealth University (VCU) in Richmond for my Bachelor of Science in Interdisciplinary Study with a focus on Psychology and Health and wellness. In college, I was a fitness center monitor at the Siegel Center. I worked at the gym and assisted individuals with working out and using the machines properly. I enjoyed the gym and working out. I liked to interact with everyone and hear about everyone's journey to gaining a healthy lifestyle. This intrigued me and led me to pursue a different passion.

A project that I undertook in college that I'd consider quite a big deal was a manifestation of my dad's favorite quote: planning. I have always been a very organized person; I am very strategic and like to plan what occurs around me if it's within my control. I don't like my feelings to be hurt or affected, so usually I will take on the extra stress to be in control so that I can protect myself. That's a hard role to play when you have other people also to protect. When in high school, I had a project in which I had to plan the rest of my life. I had to note how I wanted the rest of my life to be. I was very particular, and although this was just a project, I took it very seriously. I was never able to control what I wanted to do or when I wanted to do it, so I was very excited to begin focusing on my future.

I also have my master's in public health from Capella University, and I studied towards my doctorate in Health Administration also, but I did not finish due to trying to discern between my next path and the program ending. So, I'd say that that's what I'm currently doing. I want to do something too, where I can offer services to anyone in need. So, I think consulting is the thing I want to continue to add to it. I want to be able to help those around me. I want to be a mentor. I want to be that supportive person. I don't want to be limited to one area in life. I want my life experiences and my knowledge; to be able to learn and adapt, as well as help those around me reach their goals.

I established my business by working in this field and loving my job. I enjoyed the interactions I made with my clients and loved their transition, change, and growth through their different phases. This prompted me and my husband to partner to develop our own program.

Does the accumulation of this knowledge and degrees translate to definite answers as to who I am? I'm always trying to figure out who I am. Maybe that will never end.

I have a lot of fulfilling moments, especially with family. I enjoy family gatherings in general. There is never a dull moment; if you are going through something after seeing and interacting with your family, you can conquer whatever is bothering you head-on. I enjoy the little things like taking the kids out for their different activities, watching movies while munching on popcorn and ice cream, or our favorite family snack –chips.

Oftentimes, however, I live in my own mind wondering what I can do for people to make sure that they don't hurt me instead of figuring out how I am not going to hurt myself and how I am going to stay true to what I want to do. I learned never to let negativity change you.

Don't try to seek revenge when you are hurt, don't mock the actions of others. Just be you. Be you at all times – through the positive and negatives.

So, something that I've learned along the way that I now tell myself is that I am the brand and, as such, decided who I want to be. I am my own best image so it's up to me to make the decision; to make myself feel better. Once I heal from within, then I will enjoy life. My decisions will help dictate where I go. I continue to mope and pout that I won't get where I want to get in life. I mean, the lessons and trials and tribulations that I've been through, I need to use them as motivations to move forward and to help other people around me.

I'm in a field where I come across a lot of different situations, but a lot of which I can relate to. That may be why I'm good at my current profession. I can relate to a lot of situations. I'm adaptable. I'm able to understand. Mostly, I would like to make people aware of the need to "trust the process." If you are focused and believe in yourself, then it is only right to allow yourself and trust yourself enough to be happy and fulfilled. Cut off things that are holding you back.

Never sell yourself short. You may always be busy, but as long as you're helping others and loving what you're doing, you can't go wrong.

CHAPTER TWO
DISTRACTIONS

Distractions are things that redirect one's attention from the center of focus. It is the magician's greatest asset. It is said that magic, and its wow effect mostly happens because we focus so much on the theatrics of the performer rather than each other movement they are making. In essence the audience is made to believe that something huge is happening when in reality, it has nothing to do with the trick. It's only that the magician is skillful enough to direct an audience's attention where they want it to go. This is simply what distraction is.

The experience of being unintentionally distracted from an intended focus is likely to be frustratingly familiar to most people, and such distraction can prove highly disruptive in a variety of daily life contexts –education, the workplace, or while driving.

Indeed, in daily life, people may often be distracted by stimuli seemingly entirely unrelated to the task that they are currently engaged in. For example, a student may be distracted from studying by the sight of a friend walking by. In addition, task-irrelevant distractions may come from the external environment and internally generated stimuli associated with mind-wandering. For example, a student may be distracted from reading an assigned article by the intrusion of thought about an unrelated issue – perhaps some salient recent event in their daily life.

Distractions take attention away from what an operator needs to do when performing a task. This implies a lack of focus or a grasp of the full picture. When this happens, the dynamics of reality as we know it becomes altered based on what we've glued our eyes to. Because of this, many of us draw improper conclusions and become riddled by understanding the true synergy of how things took place.

Every now and then, we all need or could use a few distractions. But we must recognize that is what it is –nothing more. However, often, we find that people are more productive when the ping of their phones is muted or when the door is shut fully rather than leaving it dancing on its hinges. These, and many more, alter concentration.

The reality of one's focus, energy, and emotions being redirected from the centerpiece of our lives is rather a big deal. And it happens to most of us. It feeds on the loop, chip after chip, until we can no longer keep track of our progress.

Most of the time, it shouldn't even get as deep as this, but people are so moment-driven that they forget their foundation. When I say moment driven, I mean how so many have judged their results, and progress by the simplest of moments. Ordinarily, we should be able to pick on the moments that we want to shape our lives. Lack of employment and having too much time on one's hands doesn't mean that one should do almost anything, including resorting to crime.

It's what separates being moment-driven from driven moments. Driven moments are much more intentional. This is synonymous with my dad's quote on planning. With plans and schedules, driving oneself through 21 days of cultivating a habit is much easier. Otherwise, the news would pop on the phone or television screen, and a new movie would be coming to the cinema close to town. They are opposites to distractions. It, however, isn't something most people know. And that's scary.

This is one of my major fears regarding love, relationships, and life generally. Moment-driven actions alter trust in our conclusions. At these moments, the norm is rejected or pushed to the darkest of corners in our subjective minds. But moments are what they are, and there will always be many more of such offering distractions on a platter.

This may not be a big deal when we talk about harmless distractions such as hearing the kids mess the whole room up playing while I write these words. But it could be more if we consider *how* it alters human attention and thought and sometimes piles up its own bags in what appears as a watermark in our minds.

In this chapter, I will be sharing with you several instances with illustrations of how I was distracted in so many ways and what those distractions were. You might need to look into these and check if they are not what affects you too from being your best at the moment.

Distractions vary. But the endgame could ruin even the most successful people. This is because they sometimes forget. Forgetting what's important for a bigger or even a smaller moment is mind-altering. While making mistakes are temporary habits, they can always occur again. The first step is changing one's mindset to know your limits and stabilize your mistake. Admitting your faults does not allow your faults to be viewed at every encounter. The past can't be forgiven until addressed and understood.

In my everyday life, I've realized that distractions lead to exhaustion. It causes us to draw faulty conclusions because our attention isn't in one place. It tempts us to believe that certain behaviors will lead to outcomes that they certainly won't create. It prevents us from rightly understanding cause and effect, frustrating us as we are continually thwarted from getting what we desire.

Distractions vary, yet again, each offers something, albeit temporary and fleeting. Take power, for instance, it offers security but doesn't ensure or guarantee it. Some of the most powerful people in the world are often too insecure. Insecurity sometimes flames extravagance, the need for competition, and jealousy. Fame and money is neither better when we consider the promise of an easy life. Technology also promises ease of access to the rest of the world and productivity with work. However, these have evolved into some of the top distractions when discussing productivity in the workplace, success, peace, and fulfillment in life.

SHADES OF DISTRACTIONS

Distractions can be external (such as noise) or internal (such as fatigue, rumination, or stress). Distractions may be caused by several factors, including the loss of interest in the primary activity, inability to pay attention due to various reasons, or intensity of the distractor.

Every distraction or interruption that derails your productivity can be sorted into categories, depending on whether the distraction is annoying or fun and whether you have control over it. First, the distractions we can't control. It's helpful to realize there are distractions we can't control—ones that are both annoying (office visitors, loud colleagues, required meetings), and those that are fun (your coworker asking if you'd like to join the team for lunch). The key to dealing with these derailments isn't to prevent them from happening—their very nature prevents you from doing so. Instead, it's up to you to change how you respond—quickly getting back on track after annoying interruptions and enjoying any fun interruptions that happen to arise.

The distractions that we can't control, on the other hand, could include emails, phone calls, audible and vibrating alerts, text messages, social media, news websites, and the internet.

CASE STUDY I

Of these, however, the greatest distraction comes from our involvement in what is going on in other people's lives. Nothing distorts our thinking, confuses our direction, and leads us down a destructive path like our fixation on others. This is not to negate family or friends or the act of lending a hand to those in need. Rather, it's to demand that we be conscious of how much we give and take in return from such interactions.

Everything around me and in my life has always been a distraction. I like to pay attention to details, but sometimes I pay attention to other people around me too hard. This, in return, makes me lose focus on myself. I love the fact that whatever problem is discussed with me gets solved by all means since I always give it my all. In return, however, I get lost in answering my personal calls and life details.

While as a kid and growing up, it was easier being selfless or lending a hand when a friend or family member needed help with something. As an adult, it gets harder to maintain a balance with things that relate to me personally. In the midst of this also comes having to deal with everything in the lives of others, being defined not by what they have but by what they have in comparison to oneself.

With a mind altered from what is, one could have the greatest job ever and be making more money than imagined, but if a co-worker becomes the boss or someone finds out someone else is making more money, they can quickly dislike the job. I also usually pay attention to what people in my circle do. I love protecting whoever is in my circle. I hate seeing them in pain or suffering, and this often causes me to lose focus on what's needed for me to be okay. I find joy in helping others, and this is my peace. In my life, it got to a point where it was very hard for me actually to engage in normal day-to-day activities. It became tough to live a life or even go after my dreams because I felt like I had to watch out for everyone at the same time. I had to make sure that those around me were okay so that they could carry on with their dreams, even though this fixation slowed down on my own.

From the backdrop of all this, it became very hard for me actually to live fully; to go after my dreams because I felt like I had to take care of my home. It's always so much that I want to make sure that everyone is straight before I can just leave. I never want those I'm closest to have to call on someone else. I want to be everyone's go-to person. Many a time, I have gotten hurt by people close to me the most. It sometimes might mean being taken for granted, while at some other times, people simply exploit me for not always wanting to say no to their requests.

It should be said that some people often do not attribute to your positive spirit. Sometimes others judge you before giving you a chance to be your whole self, which often causes you not to trust others and hold back who you are. When you encounter something like this, distance yourself because this is not good for your mental health and well-being. Those whose negative associations continually serve as constant distractions to one's goals and dreams, and ultimately – it takes away from your happiness.

Have you ever met someone that almost seems to feed on the attention of others? They might act halfway normal for a time, but periodically they must pull a stunt to draw the attention of everyone around them just to make themselves feel better. It's such a common occurrence that almost everyone has met someone like that in their life. You must watch out for these people more than anything else. They are the king or queen of distractions and a literal siphon that absorbs your happiness into an abyss, never to be seen again.

Unfortunately, being everyone's go-to person has caused me to go through many trials and tribulations. I have had to stay glued to heart monitors, and my family does not even know. I've had four miscarriages, had my thyroid removed, and my blood pressure rose over 200 for weeks at a time. I have been at risk of a stroke, and the list continues. I have been through these thousands of things at the age of 34. And these are not good signs. I eventually realized that I had let distractions and other people's actions control my life. I must control myself and my own feelings. This is all attributed to being very strong-willed and independent. I am very focus-driven and sometimes put my goals before my feelings and health. I have learned that if you are built to be strong, then that's instilled in you, and no one can take that away. You can make time for yourself and get back to your goals when ready. Breaks are necessary!!!

If I could do things differently, it would be to cut off some work and allow those in certain positions at work to do their jobs rather than stepping in. I have surpassed many moments and not allowed attention to be given to me in my most vulnerable moments. Over time, I have learned to stick to my plan and watch how things will always work out, to remove myself from what is not an asset, from what is toxic and holding me back from reaching my goals.

CASE STUDY II

Have you ever been in a situation where you have to wonder what your significant other is doing on their phone or whom they are texting while you're there? You may at first both be on your phone at one point, but when you put down your phone, you find yourself trying to figure out who they're still texting. It begs the question of unnecessary things even to be worried about. While they're there with you, you should be focused on their presence at that moment rather than on things beyond your control. You should ask yourself, "Is your fixation on that which you have no control over building up your insecurities or improving trust in the relationship?"

The truth is, when we focus on the actions, attitudes, and outcomes of others, we create false conclusions and doubts, waste valuable time, and miss the opportunity to love or serve them wholeheartedly. We can't love those we judge. In much the same way, we can't serve others when we are jealous of them.

Also, with the prevalence of so many distractions, life just gets so scary and hard. It becomes hard to trust and enjoy the moment. Thus, it gets hard for you to let your guard down and even harder for you to even pay attention to what you're meant to be focused on. You never know what's going to happen. One moment you have the resolve to read all day, but when the day comes, a call from anyone could have you rethink that schedule you made a week earlier.

That's a major issue many individuals have with playing multiple roles. This is mostly because we know that in the roles we play, we'll have to commit to each one, but it's hard to feel or fulfill everything someone has going on. Something will definitely slide when we want to do that.

No one wants to be replaced by anyone or anything for something they love. I've stopped so many of my goals trying to make sure that everyone in my life was comfortable. I've had so many opportunities but didn't pursue them because I was scared, either scared of being hurt or condescending to because of how it'd affect those closest to me. I'm creating problems before it even happens. Now it's time for me to take advantage of my life.

So, it's scary, so scary. Life is not in our control, but we are in control of what we allow to take us out of character.

The lesson learned is that those whom you surround yourself with would be either assets or annoyances. Choose wisely.

CASE STUDY III

Have you ever had to go somewhere but couldn't do so because you didn't have the money? Even when everybody around you had the money… you're stranded but trying to avoid being sidelined. You're there trying to figure out what you should do. Did you have to use an overdraft? Did you have to make up an excuse that you couldn't come or act like you weren't hungry just to avoid anyone realizing what was happening? Anything at all to avoid the look on their faces. Many of those things have happened to me, and people would never even know.

I would never allow these things just to happen, but we are human, and some things happen. Some things are beyond my control, but now that I am in control, I will never be in those situations again if I can control them due to the pain and strife I felt when I was at my lowest point. My account was hacked several times. I'm a business owner and have had to go above and beyond to do multiple things because of this. I heard people talk about me, saying that I did things or didn't do things on purpose because I still wear nice clothes, not knowing that those clothes were things I bought three or four years ago. People judge you without knowing your story rather than asking. Presentation is everything. We are always our own brand, and you feel as you are. Every day I take pride in making sure I am presentable because you never know when you will get the chance to inspire the next person. So, it was very hard. People won't believe you, though, but try to take advantage of you instead.

While some of us are very forthcoming, I'm a person who, if I don't know about something, then I can't speak on it. Also, if I make a mistake, I'll let you know I made a mistake. I have no problem apologizing. I'm not a person who learned to just throw things under the rug. I like to come up with a solution, realize the problem, and try fixing it. But it's hard for me to deal with people sometimes, so I kind of stay to myself and only stick within my circle. Making new friends is hard for me because people sometimes have a motive and are not as forthcoming and genuine.

As we go through life struggles, we often dwell on the "what ifs" and what we don't have. The absence of that, if noticed around you, is only but a manifestation of how much some live their life riding on the fumes of others' acceleration. Fixation on others has several negative consequences in our lives. Whenever we focus on others, we take our focus off our own responsibilities. We try to change them while failing to do the work necessary to change us. Among the many problems of focusing on others, the greatest may be that we cannot rightly interpret what's going on in other people's lives. For example, when I am hurt or sad, I often focus on the people involved rather than the underlying root of what caused me to be sad. This usually ruins my entire day or week, and I am fixated on revenge or making others feel my pain because I'm stuck in a rut. This is a flaw that most of us have and continue to work on daily. I am a person who loves hard in all aspects of life, so to be hurt takes over my entire body. *Refocus* is something that I feel we as humans need to work on daily as we become more mindful of our actions.

In essence, it's important that we recognize the process that comes naturally to us. That is mostly a "focus on yourself!" Fixating on others is, in fact, toxic. Nothing good will come from comparing our lives to the lives of those around us. When we avoid this distraction, we are far more likely to make wise choices, better understand cause and effect, and relate with others in a healthy manner.

CASE STUDY IV

Another major type of distraction is yourself. This is one that I wake up to every day. I am truly a very passionate person about everything that I engage with. Whether it be work, my family, my friends, any commitment that I have. I often self-sabotage because I truly care about the outcome of life and what I encounter. This is something that most of us often have no idea what we are doing. We often place ourselves on a pedestal and then talk ourselves down to the bottom step by step. This then leads to setbacks. The lack of ability to put energy into oneself is something we as individuals do daily when we focus on the world around us before ourselves.

While it is said that distractions eat away at one's time and attention like parasites, we can also be the host. What you give room for, water, and nurture will continue to grow. If that's you, and it's most of us, it's time to start fresh and do a good cleanse occasionally. Not just an internal cleanse but an external cleanse of all environmental stressors that have caused you not to be your full self. Sometimes you must identify what caused you to be sad, to be tired, to be "stuck," and to be honest. Being honest doesn't mean you're weak, it actually means you are strong. It takes very strong individuals to admit opportunities missed and to take accountability for what is causing them to be all they can be. Distractions aren't necessarily your fault but managing them is your responsibility.

Sometimes I get scared of myself. I don't know what my actions are going to be when I get in different situations. Because of this, I sometimes get surprised by how calm I become when certain revelations or shocking experiences find their way to me. This is because life has been so hard for me in certain times, and it doesn't help much getting worked up. Also, since the solutions are often mine to discover, I'd always need a calm mind to do that. There are moments in which I can't control how I feel, and I am not ready to reveal what is causing me stress. This causes me to go in overload. As individuals who have busy lives, overthinking is something that occurs daily. Overthinking is my defense mechanism. For example, in my daily life, if I have a meeting that runs over and two of my four children have mandatory practice at the same time…what do you do? You can cancel, or they both can be late, and you can make yourself available for an extra private session to gain what was missed. This is something that occurs daily in my life. Living an unpredictable lifestyle causes many things not to go as planned daily. I used to stress myself every day when this happened, but currently, I have come to accept that I am only one person. I am dedicated, committed, and loyal, but I am not a superhero. I may have superwoman tendencies….hahaha…but working on overload and rushing is very unhealthy.

At the end of the day, what will make you happy and give you a sense of fulfillment is whether you did your best. If I gave it my all, and everyone is smiling, healthy, and safe, then nothing else matters. I tried….and that's the bottom line. Even after a day or weeks or months of trying it often leads you to go home as the "superwoman" or "superhero" you are and scream, cry in the shower and then get out with a smile and grab a glass of wine and smile as you put your children to sleep. This is something that we go through as women, we are looked upon as the person to save the day and handle everything. Sometimes we need the same grace we give those around us. For me personally, if I cry, it's a big deal so I often keep it to myself. But crying sometimes is like a detox, you let it out and come out stronger and have a clear mind. Unpredictability is the gift and the curse of life that keeps us on our toes, but this also allows for creativity.

It begs the question of whether you did everything you could to advance your career? To live your passion? To be present for your loved ones and become someone that others can place their trust in? Although these all are good questions…the main question is …WHAT DID YOU

DO FOR YOU?

> *Naturally, when we live in our own heads rather than trust the process, this becomes a new reality for us. The reality is meeting the needs of those we love and not understanding that to be the loving person that friends and family know, we still have to develop and engage in habits that make us love ourselves.*

Distractions will pull us away from realizing many things and away from our own potential. Although we like to convince ourselves that we have everything under control despite these distractions, the reality is that we sometimes need to regroup and just let go. What is meant to be will be. Life is the unpredictability that causes us to become our true selves, it opens doors of creativity for us to survive in the world.

Sometimes, I don't know who I can trust. I don't know who's watching, who's paying attention, who's going to use how I live my life against me because there's something that they are trying to achieve. This is more like dancing on the edge of paranoia, and I hate how this makes me feel these days because I'm not that way at all. I really don't care what others think because I am my own person, but I do not like my character to be assassinated. I am a very loyal person and very nonjudgmental, but the world often causes me to lose sight of my true purpose. This is because I am human. I am learning and have learned to embrace change. Embrace the unknown and focus on your abilities and what you can produce.

It should be noted that when distraction becomes a habit, we become unable to sustain the focus required for creativity in our professional and personal lives. Worse, if we are constantly pulled away from friends and family by distractions, we miss out on cultivating the relationships we need for our psychological well-being.

There at times when I should be proud, say from accomplishments and things that I should have achieved, but I feel like I'm putting a lot of pressure on myself and sometimes you're reaching out for help. But you don't know how to get that help without having others around you worried. Sometimes being strong you aren't looked upon as the priority.

You are often seen to be able to tackle any and everything regardless of whether you ask for help. This has caused me to perfect multitasking to be sure I can maintain everything that comes by way. I am that person sometimes that needs help and sometimes I don't know how to ask. I like for those around me to step in and be assertive when they think help is needed. And it's okay for me to have those feelings, Because no one's perfect. We also must remember that no one knows help is needed unless you say it...so there is another point as strong women we have to learn to communicate our needs.

CASE STUDY V

Whether to choose to do things or let your mate do things more is another major debate in the minds of many women. Have you ever had to says "sure, go… I don't have plans" or "I don't want to do anything" but you actually do want to get out of your normal routine? As a woman, it's hard to come to a happy medium sometimes without sacrifices. This is something we do have to start speaking up for. We can't be enabling. We have to set up our lives in a way that'd make us prosper as individuals and in partnerships. Without this, we cannot be the best wife, girlfriend, sister, cousin, mother, aunt, niece, granddaughter, or friend. I have done this plenty of times. In my current lifestyle, I have many goals but sometimes I am not sure how to put them into action and I am still figuring it out. If my husband has something to do and achieve and its concrete, then I often don't even mention what I have in the works. I have found that this has caused me to become resentful and often downplay my own level of worth and value. Playing multiple roles is very hard and I have found as a woman of multiple roles, the assertiveness from your partner is key in order to help keep you focused and feeling special and one of a kind, while you tackle the daily challenges. Distractions do more than hurt our productivity. They make it harder to stick to our goals and often keep us from living a happier life. Whether you have big goals you're trying to accomplish or just want to live better, you can't afford to let these distractions consume your goals and dreams for your mate's.

Although I'm a laid-back person, I really like to have fun. I'm very outspoken. I like to do things with no structure most of the time when I'm off and I like to go with the flow. However, I have not seen that side of me in a while, actually over five years. I really want to be able to show it, but I don't know how sometimes in the life that I live. Being a mother of four, a wife, and a business owner is very hard sometimes. You want to lead by example and must be responsible. Balance is the key and being able to show my kids that I am human is what is needed in my life. It's okay to be vulnerable and not strong all the time. So, I'm trying to live through my kids lol. This is the life of motherhood, but I am not only a mother, I am ..ERICA. I live through my kids. However, this has caused me major stresses, made me feel bad for myself and regret how I tackle certain situations and focus on the past. It's about time to focus on balance and how putting yourself first can help you heal and become the best version of yourself for you and those around you. Thus, recently, I am taking all the time necessary to survey my own life, to identify which of the distractions is most prevalent, and start there.

CASE STUDY VI

Another distraction. Being worried that your loved ones will be affected by your actions.

Although similar to the earlier case study on placing one's goals and plans second to those of one's mate, this extends to friends, family, colleagues at work, and so on…

You can never please everyone and that's a problem I deal with every day. We're often not trying to please people at the onset but trying to make sure everyone is okay; to control the situation beforehand and all, is just that. But we never can be there for everyone, and I must live with that. I need to know that it's okay if I can't, and that they can use other people to get things taken care of.

I never want those I'm closest to, to have to call on someone else before solving their challenges. I want to be everyone's go-to person but being everyone's go-to person has caused me to go through many trials and tribulations. There are many situations I experienced that were unknown to my family. I battled with depression and sicknesses that they weren't aware of. I have had to wear heart monitors when I battled with the stress of working hard, never having a break or downtime for me. Even on vacation, work continues. I have had plenty of vacations yet none of them have been on a schedule. I have four children and have never had maternity leave even for one day. Sticking to a schedule and routine has caused me unexplainable stress that can't be reversed.

My family did not know of the negative thoughts I had nor the lack of motivation and self-worth. None knew of the internal struggles I was having battling at the time. So many things to mention that are countless – or rather, thousands of things that had put me at the risk of danger at the age of 34 and that were not good. Each of these conditions have caused me to suffer from extreme anger, anxiety, and depression for the past five years.

The reality is that while trying to get into other people's life while having to deal with my own life at work or home, I became so stressed without even realizing it. It gets so bad to the point where I hurt my own feelings and want to start blaming it on other people. These days, I live by a to-do list. I usually end my day very late. I stay up late to send emails, purchase items for the house and kids so that I can ensure the next day runs smoothly. I have a date night each week. I don't have my computer out anymore when lying in bed. I also plan activities for my kids so that I can ensure they can take care of what they need to enjoy themselves.

So, you know, I want people to know that there are other methods of dealing with those distractions. Take that risk if you have something to do, put down the phone or other distractions. Make sure your bills are paid. If you are in a dark place, make arrangements, and go ahead to talk to someone; take care of yourself. Do something for yourself and then be sure you take care of what you need to take care of because it can't wait. Don't wait. Don't put yourself last. Do what makes you happy and enjoy yourself! Don't set limits on your happiness and treat yourself like you treat those around you…with the utmost care and love.

HOW TO MANAGE DISTRACTIONS

The solution to dealing with distractions is mostly simple. Eliminate the interruptions ahead of time. If you frequently stumble into productivity potholes while on the internet, disconnect while doing your most important work. If checking email is eating away at your productivity, or email alerts are preventing you from focusing on your work, disable those beeps and bloops, and turn off the new message notifications that pop into the corner of your screen as you're working. Schedule a few windows throughout the day to intentionally check your email, instead of checking it habitually.

On most occasions, however, these are not as easy are they are made to sound. Here are a few go-to tips:

- **Setting Your Day Up Ahead**

I recommend setting your main objectives every day. It's so easy to give in to distraction if you have a long list of things to achieve in a day, or if you have none. I personally love to prepare for my day ahead. Without such a thing as a to-do list and goal sheet, I believe I'd have given in to days I feel the urge to give up even before starting. I admit that it's best to limit your daily goals by writing down at least three main objectives and paste them in a visible place. This will give you a clearer mind on what to focus more on and then you can proceed to work on those things that are less important after you've accomplished your major objectives.

Before I started doing this, I found that I had shorter days. It was always almost as if I was running against time. And it's crazy how time can fly when you don't plan ahead. By nightfall, I'd find myself still carrying my work to bed, and probably waiting till sleep calls to me while trying to get things done. Recently however, I don't carry work to bed, and I tend to accomplish more despite having to deal with four kids. I also plan my children's day ahead – there are days to go strolling in the park; to go on dates as well, and so on.

Simply put, convert your values into practical steps. Values include attributes of the person you want to become. They include being a contributing member of a team, being a loving parent, being in an equitable marriage, seeking wisdom, taking care of your physical fitness, or being a generous friend. By making time for them in your day through planning your schedule, it is only a matter of time before they start reflecting in your personal life.

- **Break Things Down –Both Time and Things to Get Done**

It never hurts to work with a shorter time frame when it comes to daily schedules and even longer goals. According to Parkinson's Law, "work tends to expand to fill the time we have available for its completion." Give yourself a shorter deadline to finish your work and get a backup plan to hold yourself accountable. This will help you avoid distractions and improve your productivity because when we're up against a deadline, we suddenly become laser focused and avoid distractions at all costs.

- **Distraction-free Mode**

This is that mode I enter to get the best of my day and record more personal progress on my goal sheet. I simply put myself in a position where it is less likely for me to get preoccupied with something other than what I am supposed to be working on at the moment. This starts with closing the door to my room or office, or I just locate a quiet spot in the house when the kids are out playing or with an aunt. You could zone out also with noise-canceling headphones. During these times, you could either turn off your phone or put it on silent and move it away from you so you can't pick it up easily.

I encourage and find peace in keeping the phone far away because it gets straining to stand up from within a schedule to check a notification or pick up a call. Most times, I just leave the phone to do its vibration dance while I call back later. The idea here is simply to cherish this little room or mode and protect it from even a minute of distractions.

- **Negotiate Boundaries**

Most of us easily get pulled out of the center of our lives into the middle of other people's. It could be at work or with family and friends. We need to learn to negotiate our boundaries with people. Make them realize that we are self-centered when it comes to the pursuit of specific personal goals. This enables us to look after our own interests and stand up for ourselves, while letting other people know where they stand. By making your expectations of others clear and direct, as well as disentangling from co-dependent relationships without getting caught up in other people's dramas or intense emotions, distraction is grossly reduced. Now, this is a gem of a solution. You must even set boundaries in your own household. You must voice your opinions and how you feel and stand firm about what makes you feel unworthy.

- **Monitor Your Mind and be able to Recall it to Order**

This here just might be the toughest nut to crack, especially since it requires a strong internal focus. Pay attention to your thoughts and recognize when your mind starts wandering or is triggered. This will allow you to know and control what to focus on and help bring your thoughts back to your work. Know what distractions are hard to avoid, so you can catch them sooner. When you feel your mind wandering and getting distracted, take a deep breath and choose not to react to it.

- **Break the Cycle of Stress**

At the start of every problem with concentration or distraction is exhaustion. This is yet another internal trigger. Stress and anxiety can make one feel exhausted, easily distracted, and unable to focus. Thus, it is recommended to bring your stress level down and under control. You could do this by finding ways to calm your mind and relax your body to reduce the body's stress response, get enough sleep, practice some breathing exercises, and find ways to contain your anxiety. This will help you focus more and prevent distractions easily. The knowledge from my working in the gym has somewhat taught me to be more physical when managing stress and sleeping well. So, even with a few stretches, I feel more energized to work and handle chores.

CHAPTER SUMMARY

Overall, distractions affect the foundation of goals, aspirations, and trust. While positive thinking may determine one's perception of things around them and, at the same time, redirect energy, it often helps individuals to stay focused in all settings. Many people make excuses when they feel down, but they often have to focus on what caused them to be distracted and how to dissolve the negativity with positive factors. When I am overwhelmed or think about something that makes me frustrated, I try to engage in something that intently changes my attitude or way of thinking. This can be anything from spending time with my family, friends, going out to eat, grabbing drinks, shopping, or traveling. Goal setting is a huge factor many people often have difficulty establishing. This is sometimes attributed to their lack of ability to focus on one task at a time. Rather than setting long-term goals, I set short-term goals. Due to having a busy lifestyle, I usually set weekly goals. By doing this, it reduces the pressure and helps me to reach them more often. This helps ensure that I can reach my goals without making excuses.

Here are a few things I suggest doing:

- **Master your internal triggers.**
This involves understanding what drives your behavior – what prompts you to compulsively look at your phone or read one more email. This often includes discomforting variables such as boredom, loneliness, insecurity, fatigue, and uncertainty. Recognizing these elements makes it easier to learn to control how you react to them.

- **Convert your values into practical variables.**
Values include attributes of the person you want to become. They include being a contributing member of a team, being a loving parent, being in an equitable marriage, seeking wisdom, taking care of your physical fitness, or being a generous friend. By making time for them in your day through planning your schedule, it is only a matter of time before they start reflecting in your personal life.

- **Talk to and be around like-minded individuals.**
Be around uplifting individuals. Be around those who support you and be around those whom you are also able to learn from. By sharing experiences and allowing those you trust to guide you, you can become more comfortable as a person.

- **Negotiate boundaries.**
Most of us need to learn to negotiate our boundaries with people. This enables us to look after our interests and stand up for ourselves while letting others know where they stand. Making your expectations of others clear and direct helps to reduce any misunderstandings.

- **Manage your external triggers.**
This involves setting boundaries and knowing when to say no and when to stop.

- **Commit to the goal.**
By accepting what was and focusing on what can be, this helps to focus on progress. Progress can often be halted when we don't accept things out of our control.

Our world is full of distractions —the most dangerous are those we do not recognize.

When you eventually achieve a state where you control your impulses, do pass the baton within your network of friends, coworkers, and family to help you and look out for you. You can inspire your friends and family to pursue the lives they envision. You can also help your children learn the same by your actions.

CHAPTER THREE
FEAR OF THE UNKNOWN

Fear...how do you define fear? Fear is often learned from past experiences. How do we move past what scares us? This is often a task we go through as adults and children. As adults, fear often takes over our lives and stunts our growth. Yet, as children, we can move past and replace the memory with a fixation. Maybe it's why our childhood days are the happiest and most adventurous times of our lives. What separates our thinking from what we know over time? Our thinking… and fixation on things we do not know or have much control over. Some of my fears include failure and those around me having to ask other people for help. Helping those I love is what makes me feel good at the end of the day. No amount of money or materialistic thing gives me the same fulfillment as when I'm able to be the "go-to" person that I love. This often has caused me to let myself down. I have more expectations of myself than I do of others.

Fear, worry, and anxiety go hand in hand with the things that we know for certain will happen. At the same time, they are like complementary cards or the red and green colors that trail Christmas. More often than not, these fears and worries are justified. It is either someone – a friend, partner, or colleague at work- that puts you in a situation where you have to think about what is to come or makes you mentally break down the implications of their actions or yours. These are all fair and quite unavoidable in our everyday lives.

Yeah, it is normal to occasionally worry, have negative thoughts, or experience a sense of fear or dread about future events, obligations, or situations, especially to protect ourselves. But when these supposed reactions to thoughts, situations, and things yet to happen shape how we act or influence the ways we do not act, there is a problem.

FEAR

Fear is a natural, powerful, and primitive human emotion. It forms part and parcel of the human evolutionary process. It helps explain how wants and needs, just as survival instincts, shape development, and invention. The evolution of most world civilizations comes from the reality that there are needs to be met, albeit gradually. Certain consequences and their result of fears are not as appealing if these are not met. It is rightly a universal biochemical response, speaking from a biological standpoint, as well as a high individual emotional response. Fear alerts us to the presence of danger or the threat of harm, whether that danger is physical or psychological.

Although fear is most often in our heads, it often manifests itself physically. Sometimes, fear stems from real threats but can also originate from imagined dangers. Real threats could be based on rather complex theories derived from the experience of others. It could also be a result of our own past experiences or trauma. Fear, however, is not the same as a phobia. If you're slightly uneasy about swimming in the ocean after watching "Jaws," the movie did what it set out to do. But if you find yourself terrorized, traumatized, and unable to function at the mere thought of basking on the beach, you might be experiencing more than just fear. The difference between fear and phobia is simple. Fears are common reactions to events or objects. But fear becomes a phobia when it interferes with your ability to function and maintain a consistent quality of life. You may have a phobia if you start taking extreme measures to avoid water, spiders, or people. One thing to note is that fear is incredibly complex. And its most dangerous type is that of imagined fears. These are all in our heads.

Fear is experienced in your mind, but it triggers a strong physical reaction in your body. As soon as you recognize fear, your amygdala – a small organ in the middle of your brain goes to work. It alerts your nervous system, which sets your body's fear response into motion. Stress hormones like cortisol and adrenaline are released. Your blood pressure and heart rate increase. You start breathing faster. Even your blood flow changes — blood flows away from your heart and into your limbs, making it easier for you to throw punches or run for your life. Your body is preparing for fight-or-flight.

Have you ever wondered what the heck is about to happen, even when things are going well? You're fearing the unknown.

You know, you're creating stories because things may be going too well, and you're not sure what's going to come from this. This is synonymous with saying that your life is meant for failure. I do this so well, too. When things go well, I'm often skeptical… like, "Oh my God! Something is wrong. Somebody is not being trustworthy. I'm not sure this is real."

Doubts. Anxiety. Fears. Xenophobia.

And because of how strong these feelings are in many of us, we stay where we are, unmoving, just analyzing and breaking things down because we haven't been through situations where you know you can try or trust something to go well, just as you planned it. The master of all of the variants of fear is that it's caused by uncertainty. Fear of the unknown is the foundation of what makes us uncertain enough as we let all the other feelings and thoughts bubble to the surface.

The fear of the unknown can be hard to describe. This is mostly because all the feelings and thoughts around this fear are in our heads. These negative feelings and thoughts create mental blocks. These mental blocks influence how we live our lives and, if let loose, can have a detrimental impact on us living our lives to the fullest. When we choose to live with our fear of the unknown, our choices and decisions do not serve us well. Any decision we make based on this fear will not be a decision that will move us forward in life.

At so many points, the fear of the future and of things I'm yet to experience were the determinants of the choices I made. They shaped the way I think of the world, how I live, and even how I relate to everything and everyone around me. For example, when a close aunt of mine passed away, it hurt me deeply. My family did not know that I had failed two classes and I had withdrawn from the semester. I continued to go to school and take other courses, even though it didn't count. I could never bring myself to tell my family I failed out of school. I had never gotten anything less than a "c" in school, so getting an "f" made me feel horrible. Through time I grieved and re-evaluated my goals. I returned to school and switched my curriculum to reflect everything I was interested in.

We all have different levels of intolerance to the uncertainty that comes with unfamiliar things, which is a naturally developed characteristic. Individuals with high levels of intolerance to uncertainty might find unknown or uncertain situations almost unbearable or have an inability to cope, thus impacting their ability to function. Sometimes, a fear of the unknown can be closely related to a fear of change. Lack of predictability and control can be a contributing factor to fear. If little information is available to predict an outcome or make a decision, this can increase one's feelings of anxiety and uncertainty.

SHADES OF FEAR

Fear is never alone. We always hope along with it that the thing we are afraid of will not happen. Everyone, in one way or the other, is caught in between the loop of fear and hope. Fear and hope are accompanied by knowledge and ignorance. Having knowledge of the object we fear usually brings us to the doors of hope, while ignorance and its unknown variables exhibit fear on most occasions. It could be said that death is the only fear with a guaranteed sense of knowledge.

The fear of the unknown, also known as xenophobia, or defined by what many call uncertainties, is the simple manifestation of "what you don't know really can hurt you." Xenophobia? Yes, that one. It can also be interpreted to mean the fear of strangers or foreigners — but its original meaning is much broader. It includes anything or anyone that's unfamiliar or unknown. Researchers define fear of the unknown as the tendency to be afraid of something you have no information about on any level. For some people, fearing the unknown can go a step further.

Xenophobia is the most extreme fear of the unknown. It refers to when some people have irrational thoughts and beliefs about people and situations that they perceive to be strange or foreign. Essentially it is the fear of anything that is beyond their comfort zone. While we are not necessarily xenophobic or commit violent crimes against other people out of fear, we do, however, let our fear of the unknown rule our lives. If we listen to our fear of the unknown, we choose to live our lives in our comfort zone rather than taking up the opportunity to step out into the unknown. When you step out into the unknown, you truly start to live your life to the fullest.

If you feel intensely upset and anxious when encountering an unfamiliar situation, you may have developed a state of mind called "intolerance of uncertainty." This means uncertain circumstances feel unbearable to you.

From studies and experience, the fear of the unknown has different intensities. The different levels of fear can also be determined by the situation or based on one's personality traits, such as temperament, past experiences, trauma, or the ability to adapt and cope. Or the almost harmless low levels of fear characterized by dislikes towards something or when something becomes a bother. At this stage, our fear of the unknown is the type of one's partner, friends, or family simply brushing aside with soothing words of comfort. They either provide relief to us through their validations or just provide listening ears so we don't continue to munch on these fears. One of the kids may be fighting at school, or one's partner may be spending too much time at work and less with the family. This form of fear comes with positions or a sense of responsibility. One's boss at work can't help but worry about how effective the other staff are in their different roles. As such, a mother cannot but worry about her kids' safety at school or the playground.

A more intense shade of the fear of the unknown is the moderate levels of fear. This goes together with general fearfulness or intolerance towards things. This is the most common and natural of all the fears of the unknown. It comes with learning a new language or skill like bungee jumping for the first time despite one's fear of heights or picking up a new job. These all come with their attendants of uncertainties. But they are normal. One learning a new language would question the sanity of his decision and could either proceed to become an expert or could as well proceed to say that he/she cannot do it. From the first step, one about to jump from a height would imagine himself leaping off and falling to his death and as such, would be meticulous and wary of every string and belt. These are all normal. Regardless of how normal these are, they could translate into chronic fears when given the room to fester.

The final and most severe of these fears is the high levels of fear marked by terror or dread. This is extreme and often caused by trauma from past experiences or real life-threatening situations. Chronic fear of the unknown (also known as xenophobia) can become problematic and begin impacting your emotional, social, and physical life as seriously as any phobia might.

WHY WE FEAR THE UNKNOWN
Our fear of the unknown is natural, as highlighted earlier. It is part of our DNA. It is an essential part of our survival. This fear will often protect you and heighten your sense of threatening situations. This is a good fear to listen to. Then there is the fear that paralyzes you and stops you from living life to the fullest. This is the fear that you need to understand why it exists within you.

The fear of the unknown is made up of many thoughts and beliefs that result from negative experiences. If you have failed in business or feel you have failed in life and have low self-belief, your fear of the unknown will be heightened to protect you. When it goes beyond protection, then it should be reassessed and checked. To checkmate these fears, however, the myriad of factors that encourage or boost our fears would need to be evaluated.

What triggers the fear of the unknown in us, first and foremost, is not change or unpredictability. It is all about NOVELTY. Change has always been unpredictable to different degrees, and even if it's true that the change we are experiencing right now is getting more unpredictable by the hour, it is the absence of not having a past point of reference that is really fanning the flames of our fears. Our subconscious mind dislikes change, but more importantly, it abhors novelty — that thing that zaps us right between the eyes without knowing how to respond to it because it's completely off our records. The subconscious mind lives and thrives on patterns and keeps those patterns intact as much as possible. Of course, these patterns change over time by learning new information or experiencing more of life, but essentially, it will keep resisting anything that threatens to break those patterns. This is why freeing ourselves from old habits and patterns of behavior is so hard.

When something is totally new and is not pegged to some previous pattern of some sort, we subconsciously open up to the deepest of our fears — the fear of the unknown. And quite rightly, this time, it's not as irrational as fear either because, truth be told, novelty is the twin sister of the unknown. How we collectively understand and approach this novelty is the key to it all.

It should also be known that we all have different levels of TOLERANCE FOR UNCERTAINTY or things that we do not know. This is a naturally developed characteristic in everybody. Individuals with high levels of this intolerance may find unknown or uncertain situations almost unbearable or have been unable to cope. This greatly impacts their ability to function. Sometimes, a fear of the unknown can be closely related to a fear of change. An example of this is simply how we all react to things. If there's one thing I learned from my dad, mom, and many aunts and uncles while growing up, it's that they are somewhat receptive and welcoming to the many things I'd often find bizarre. From this, we could say that uncertainty is part of the human experience. Some people thrive in uncertain times; others become emotionally paralyzed based on how afraid they are of the unknown. The reality often is that experiences somewhat alleviate these fears. Surprises and the fear of how things would play out are never recurring situations or events. Even when they are, the way we react to them is never of fear. We can only be surprised or even have anticipated it. Here, I must agree that history is the study of the past that helps us understand the present while projecting into the future. Experience, knowledge, and familiarity come with history. The present negates fear as a would-be reaction, which forms the basis of the future and how we plan for our goals.

A third reason so many of us fear and hate venturing into the unknown is the LACK OF PREDICTABILITY and CONTROL. If there's little information available to predict an outcome or the consequences of a decision we would be making, human anxiety and feeling of uncertainty would continue to rise.

At various times, I've felt VULNERABLE. I'm thinking about what people would do to me in return despite giving my all. This is often a downward spiral for me, considering how on so many occasions, my trust gets broken. Ordinarily, building trust from scratch is very hard.

For me, that is almost impossible. When my trust is gone, it is hard for me. I can't forgive and continue on. It's even harder for me to really know that it's ever genuine again because I will never do that to someone. I will never hurt anyone around me. So, it's hard to actually come to terms with the fact that you can be hurt. And that's something we all must work on as individuals.

Maybe it's not the uncertainty of the unknown that fears us. Maybe it's the RISK that comes with proceeding with our lives either way. Any time we take an action with some uncertainty of outcome, we are taking a risk. And because life is so full of these uncertainties, risk becomes a necessary evil. What keeps us sane when making these decisions in the face of uncertainty is properly weighing the potential costs and benefits of each risk. If the uncertainty feels manageable, then we can feel okay about our decisions. "I've gone through years without any form of help, I can always survive on my own…" and so on is an example of such scenarios.

While that is a good scenario, when we can no longer keep a tab of the risks of an action, expectation, or event, we could say then that uncertainty has overflowed our sense of reality. The implication is that we become survivalists in every adjoining endeavor. We go back to the rudiment and its characteristic animal instinct, which assumes the worst of all and trusts in no one to protect ourselves. This is why uncertainty produces anxiety.

When we have no clue what to say to someone, we assume they will laugh at us no matter what we do. When we have given our all to someone, we either expect the best in return or just assume they are incapable of reciprocating the same. When we don't know anything about the new family in town, we tend to imagine that they are escaping something and want to keep to themselves. When we feel sick and don't know why, we immediately assume it must be Cancer of Everything. And this latter example goes so well with me. When things go too well, I become plagued by the thoughts of something good or bad coming out of this. I tend to imagine that someone was being dishonest in how happy they were about good things. It's almost always as if I was waiting for a bomb to tick off in the not-so-far distance. This is because our unconscious mind, when seeing that we don't know if something is a threat or not, goes on to assume that it is. It decides, "better the devil I know than the devil I don't."

IMPLICATIONS
Fear conquers all in most measures. Some people fear what may or may not happen. Fear is a distraction that ruins success, progression in life, and even existence.

While Destructive fear alerts us to a non-existent threat. There is no actual threat, but our minds tell us there is, explains Manly. Depending on the severity of a person's fear of change, it may become destructive. If destructive fear of the unknown is left unmanaged, potential complications may include depression, anxiety, isolation, avoidance, stress, substance use disorders, staying in unhealthy environments, staying in toxic relationships, and suicidal ideation.

There is so much ambiguity when we examine situations that tend to be uncertain and unpredictable or can cause anxiety. This anxiety is in addition to other psychological and physical problems in some populations, especially among those who engage in it constantly. For example, in war-ridden places or in places of conflict, terrorism, abuse, etc.

Poor parenting that instills fear can also impair the strength of a child's psyche development or personality. For example, there are parents that tell their children not to talk to strangers to protect them. While this is advisable in most communities, in school, they would be motivated not to show fear in talking with strangers but to be assertive and aware of the risks and the environment in which it takes place. This creates in the child rather ambiguous and mixed messages. This can, in fact, affect their self-esteem and self-confidence.

- **There is the fear of yourself and fear of expectations.**

At some point, I thought I knew my wants and needs. But sometimes, I don't. Little things bother me from observation, lack of attention, personal expectations and experiences, gratitude, wanting to be loved, and many more. These are not things one should seek, these should come.

Bonding, knowing the other person, knowing how to please them, pushing limits to ensure happiness, and maintaining the friendship. These all should come. Friendship, especially, requires trust. Trusting based on it is a bond gained from memories and experiences that will help a person manage daily struggles.

But I wonder, who do I run to or talk to? Who shows me sympathy or gives me that level of physical comfort enough just to cry and let go of my worries without being judged? Sympathy is a sense of love that manages struggles and manages the inevitable. You gain happiness when you develop a purpose for yourself and know that all your actions are self-fulfilling. Happiness is not gained upon words they are gained upon action and genuine comfort.

What connects these to the fears of the unknown is the implications of some of the things we fear; how they shape our relationships with others, with family, and with friends. Often, these fears have us second-guessing every step of the way. Sometimes I get scared of and question myself, my abilities, and my intentions. I don't know what my actions are going to be when I get in different situations. That's because I always anticipate and pre-plan things, even before they become actual situations or events. Because of this, I sometimes get surprised by how calm I become when certain revelations or shocking experiences find their way to me. At other times, the joy of surprises and accomplishments eludes me because of expectations. It's more like I count my eggs before they hatch. I can only attribute this to the fact that I put in so much work and expect life to reward me with the same.

Sometimes, it's easy to forget that at the end of the day, whether you did your best will make you happy and give you a sense of fulfillment. It's not always about the result or the future but the process. It begs the question of whether one did everything one could to advance one's career? To live your passion? To be present for your loved ones and become someone that others can place their trust in?

Naturally, when we live in our own heads rather than trust the process, this fear of what will come next becomes a new reality. Its distractions will pull us away from realizing many things and away from our own potential. Although we like to convince ourselves that we have everything under control despite these distractions, the reality is that we sometimes need to reorient ourselves for our own becoming. Sometimes, when we don't know whom we can trust, who's watching, who's paying attention, who's going to use how we live our lives against us because there's something that they are trying to achieve, this is more like dancing on the edge of paranoia, and I hate how this makes me as a person feel these days because I'm not that way at all.

- **Everything and Everyone Become Threats**

The first reaction to any form of fear is the thought that something is looming in the dark to usurp our progress, peace, happiness, family, friendships, and everything else that's good in our lives.

> *When uncertain about what's happening around us, we see our immediate environment as a threat. When we're uncertain about what will happen, we see the future as a threat. And when we're uncertain of what's going on with our body, we assume it's cancer.*

In much the same way, when we are uncertain about the people around us, or any of the previously mentioned distractions, we start to question our relationships, friendships, and goals. I've found this at the base of some of my trust issues and not living fully.

How can you recognize if you have a fear of change?

There are many distinct characteristics of the fear of change that someone might experience in their everyday life. Some of these signs include feeling stuck or unhappy in a situation yet avoiding creating positive change, staying in a failing relationship despite wanting to leave, or refusing or not wanting to strive for an ideal career when you are miserable in your current one. Also, these fears manifest when you have extreme anxiety over what will happen in your future or are unable to accept life changes that are within or outside of your control. In such instances, most people refuse to stray from an everyday routine because they are uncertain of what will happen if they don't stick to it. They reject invitations to events, celebrations, family or friends' homes. They could also be manifested in heart palpitations, mood swings or transferred aggression, shaking uncontrollably, and sweating profusely.

- **Overestimating Threats or Situations**

In everyday life, we must often decide whether to accept or reject impending risk. Naturally, the way we evaluate and process different options plays an important role in our fear response. Assessing the probability of a negative event helps us allocate our cognitive resources efficiently. However, many of the threats people with phobias dread the most are not based on an objective risk. Some of these are often grossly exaggerated.

HOW TO WORK ON THESE FEARS

Fear is sometimes considered the opposite of courage. However, this is incorrect. Because courage is a willingness to face adversity, fear is an example of a condition that makes the exercise of courage possible. This means that fear should not be viewed as a defective or simply protective intuition. Instead, we should consider it as a part of living. Courage loses its relevance without the element of fear.

Often, to escape the fear of the unknown and its attendant uncertainty, most people deal with the fear of not knowing by imagining something certain. Since the anxiety of what the future promises are just too much to bear, we'd gladly trade it for certitude, albeit delusional or ignorantly deduced. Because we feel certain about something doesn't mean it's true. Actually, knowing something is true, and the feeling of knowing something is true are two different things, and one can occur without the other. To be healthy and happy, we must strike a sweet spot. We must admit that there's some uncertainty in the world because that is what will keep us open to change, allow us to learn, and help us adapt to challenges. But, at the same time, we need to feel some degree of certainty as well so that we can feel a sense of security and at least pretend we know what we're doing. Getting this supposed sweet spot isn't in any way easy.

- **No avoidance!**

First, we must stop running away from things we are uncomfortable with. The more we avoid negative emotions, the more those emotions will paradoxically screw us over at some point. In much the same way, ignoring that you're angry only causes that anger to well up and then explode at some inopportune moment – and often at the wrong person or thing. Ignoring the resentment one harbors for a partner or friend and pretending everything is fine between you only festers over time and puts a strain on your relationship that can last for years, if not your entire life.

Also, ignoring the anxiety and discomfort you feel in the face of uncertainty only worsens your anxiety towards uncertainty. Avoidance provides temporary relief, but in the long term, it can be damaging. Most modern people practice escapism from the rest of the world by burying their heads in their phones. The implication of this is that we find ourselves unable to come to terms with real-life uncertainty because we have no experience of any sort. It's like one who was never exposed to any germs of any kind. A person's immune system would never be able to fight off infections because it never "learned" how to fight off any infections. Thus, we should make ourselves more resilient towards uncertainty by sitting with uncertainty.

Another way to ensure we don't avoid these fears is by systematic desensitization or flooding. Systematic desensitization focuses on breaking us away from the known and unknown fear through gradual familiarization. Simply, one is exposed in gradual steps to those situations that we fear. For example, if you have a fear of snakes, you may spend the first session with your therapist talking about snakes. Slowly, over subsequent sessions, your therapist would lead you through looking at pictures of snakes, playing with toy snakes, and eventually handling a live snake. This is usually accompanied by learning and applying new coping techniques to manage the fear response.

Flooding on the other hand, is another technique that brings the person to recognize that their phobia is a learned behavior and one that they need to unlearn. With flooding, you are exposed to a vast quantity of the feared object or a feared situation for a prolonged time in a safe, controlled environment until the fear diminishes. For instance, if you're afraid of planes, you'd go on up in one anyway.

Both methods aim to get you past the overwhelming anxiety and potential panic to a place where you must confront your fear and eventually realize that you're OK. This can help reinforce a positive reaction (you're not in danger) with a fearful event (being in the sky on a plane), ultimately getting you past the fear.

- **Don't Doubt Yourself**

An underlying cause of our fear of the unknown is based on our fear of failure. This is especially true when we are about to embark on a new journey that will take us out of our comfort zone. If one could really understand the source of one's fear of the unknown, especially in lieu of the realistic risks of stepping out of your comfort zone, then it becomes easy to accept that failure could be an option. If you cannot accept that the possibility of failure is an option, then your fear of the unknown will convince you to stay put in your comfort zone. Actually, the fear of the unknown prefers that you don't do anything and live with regret than step out and possibly fail.

If we take away the idea of failure and use setbacks as experiences to draw lessons from, there will always inevitably be a positive outcome at some point in your journey. Simply, we must be okay with knowing that if something goes wrong, we will still be okay.

- **Expect the Unexpected Through Planning**

To reclaim your sense of agency, you can start by analyzing your circumstances and listing the things you can and cannot control. You can decrease uncertainty by making a plan that includes steps you can take in areas within your control. Once you understand where your fear of change comes from, you can set attainable goals to take actionable steps toward positive change. Our fears also tend to subside when we embrace a can-do attitude, take things one step at a time, and move toward them slowly, mindfully, and in conscientious ways. This is where my dad's motto, which I shared earlier about planning/preparation, comes into play. Planning your day, work, business, and every form of relationship means you're provided with a sense of direction and become almost ready for any surprise.

Focus. Plan your life, don't let it plan you. — **Dad**

Closely associated with this is the need to embrace change. The one thing that is constant in our lives is change. We live in a world of constant and, at times, disruptive change. The more we resist change, the more it will persist in our lives. Accept that you cannot avoid the effect of change in your life. The more we open up to and expect the concept of change, the more resilient and courageous we all become.

Resisting change keeps one in a place of discomfort, where the fear of the unknown likes to sit. Your fear will keep you paralyzed in a bad situation because it is what it knows best and where it can control you. Stepping out and embracing change will open you up to a world of opportunities and growth. With its myriad of unknown and new things, change will become a fact of life that you will embrace. Essentially, this is like building habits. The real benefit is that building healthy habits brings you face-to-face with what you can and cannot control in your life. This, in turn, makes you more comfortable with uncertainty or more at peace with your thoughts and pursuits.

Face it!
When we choose to live with our fear of the unknown, our choices and decisions do not serve us well. Any decision we make based on this fear will not be a decision that will move us forward in life. Living your life to your fullest potential can only be achieved when you have come face to face with your fear of the unknown. But this is not an easy thing to do. It is a bit more complicated than just choosing to ignore your fear of the unknown. To be able to conquer your fear of the unknown, you have to be committed to making the changes within yourself, and that is where it gets tough.

Many layers of emotions are associated with your fear of the unknown, and overcoming this fear requires you to dig deep to find the courage to step into the unknown. This is not what your fear of the unknown likes. All those deep-seated limiting beliefs will resist and fight back because your actions will challenge them and question their existence. However, once you accept that the discomfort will subside over time, then riding that wave of fear becomes much easier.

While the COVID-19 pandemic was a change no one could have anticipated, it was considered by many as an opportunity to introspect, spend more time with or create new friends and family, take on new projects, etc. I have come across the Texas Kannada Short Film Festival, where the lockdown encouraged a project to promote art, film, and stories and build cultural gaps.

A Woman's Journey

Aside from having my Irish Twin sons between February 2020 and April 2021, the lockdown helped strengthen my family. It gave us opportunities – I wouldn't say it exposed our weaknesses, but it helped identify some things we needed to work on as a family unit within my home and within ourselves. It also showed how strong my husband and I are as a team.

Live in the Moment. Enjoy the Moment. Do What You Say You're Going to Do

You can take action today to reduce the possibility of a negative outcome down the road. Listing factors within your control and then taking one small step each day can shore up your sense of responsibility and control over your life.

This is also synonymous with finding the time to sit quietly and alone, reflecting on our lives in more compassionate ways and without judgment. Paying attention to our feelings and sensations in the present moment rather than getting caught up in excessive preoccupations with the past or imagined future catastrophes.

During the lockdown, to keep our family intact and together, we identified that we needed to pay more attention to each other and what each other needs; to leave the outside on the outside and be more present in the moment with each other. Undistracted.

That was something that I really needed to work on. I have come to realize that I had a hard time dwelling on the past, analyzing and breaking moments, actions, and reactions down to see what my faults were. Often, I'd wonder where I could have been more accountable to save the situation. I had to teach myself to acknowledge that no one is perfect. The goals and tools that were instilled in me make me over analyze life so much, and I can't just live in the moment. As a family, including aunts, uncles, cousins, and everyone, we did not get together as we usually do. But we did start a family group chat where we shared pictures and everything during that time. Although we tried to stay very close but safe, we also lost several family members who were very dear to us. So, it made us recognize how you don't need to wait till someone is sick to say "I love you" or to make time to see them. We need to keep our family tight and strong and keep making those moments.

- **Your Intentions Must Be Well**

People often say, "It's the thought that counts" when they receive a gift, compliment, or favor – and this idea has a strong psychological truth. It goes beyond the recipient just being appreciative or nice enough, it is proof that the results of our actions or that of others may be irrelevant when we consider that process.

This is most true when it comes to both kind and harmful acts. Two sides of a divide. In much the same way, let's consider how much it matters to you if someone accidentally spills their drink on your new shirt or if they intentionally spill their drink on you to upset you, even if the consequences of the action itself are exactly the same. When people perceive a bad deed as intentional, they often have a stronger urge to retaliate or punish that person and seek justice. When the bad deed is unintentional, finding forgiveness and letting it go is easier.

In all cases, our intentions make a big difference. If you don't have the right intentions and you can't treat people with earnest kindness, you'll always find yourself playing "games" or "competing" to win people over and get them to like you. This would mean that you'll have to entice them with something material. The reality, however, is that whatever it is that draws people to you when it gets exhausted, you lose these people. Your relationship and connection with these people will always have you living in fear of providence or lack of something. You'd find it difficult to trust.

Authentic kindness includes being kind and respectful toward people with zero to offer you. If you can ignore judging people as "superior" or "inferior," and you can treat everyone at the same level as equals, you'll be able to flourish in almost any social situation. Perhaps this is why some research shows that kindness helps social anxiety because you're shifting the focus from "How can I help myself?" to "How can I help others?" That's a powerful reframe because it takes you out of your head and into the present moment. It also allows you to be positive minded about what to expect. Someone with a dubious intention would always have to look over their shoulders, either anticipating that they'd get caught or otherwise. That's not a way to live.

CHAPTER SUMMARY

Summarily, fear is a natural yet necessary evil. It's a cognitive ability innate to every one of us. It is there to keep us safe from whatever harm or threat there is. Well, it is normal to occasionally worry, have negative thoughts, or experience a sense of fear or dread about future events, obligations, or situations. But when these supposed reactions to thoughts, situations, and things yet to happen, shape how we act or influence the ways that we do not act, then there is a problem.

Fear of the unknown or irrational fear is caused by negative thinking (worry) which arises from anxiety accompanied by a subjective sense of apprehension or dread. Irrational fear shares a common neural pathway with other fears, a pathway that engages the nervous system to mobilize bodily resources in the face of danger or threat.

The manifestation of the fear of the unknown is seen in certain aspects of our lives. But not all of us know whether they are of positive or negative influence on us. Here are a few questions to ask:

- Is my fear of the unknown preventing me from doing things I am interested in?
- Am I isolating myself from people, places, or things because I am fearful?
- Are my relationships negatively impacted?
- Has my anxiety, fear, or depression worsened?
- Am I missing out on opportunities because I am fearful of the unknown?
- Are a majority of my thoughts and behaviors related to my fear of the unknown?

Also, some recommendations to rid ourselves of the negative hold and effects fear include:

- Avoiding avoidance as a practice is a good way to live and experience life fully.
- Being more present as against living with our 'heads in the cloud'

means that we get to experience moments as they unfold.
- Such techniques as mindfulness, meditation, and positive thinking can help reduce feelings of worry and anxiety.
- Working to increase our self-esteem, either through self-affirmation or through setting of realistic expectations is one way to know our capability and maintain agency over things that we can control.
- Engaging actively in self-care activities such as hangouts, social and leisure time, exercise, resting, all help boost mental, physical, social, and emotional health.
- Reach out. Listen to other people's experiences. Verbalize your feelings to reduce how much you worry or get anxious thinking about it on your own.
- Seek therapy, either an individual one to help process and challenge those fears or a group one where you get support and encouragement from people who have experienced the same.

CHAPTER FOUR
ACCEPTANCE

Feeling accepted and loved has never been an issue in life until now. This is a statement of fact especially since acceptance is the truth to a true bond. Accepting one another's personal gains and faults and helping each other grow is as natural as letting oxygen run its course through our lungs. But not so many of us have really reached that stage where we get to breathe. So many of us live the greater part of our lives holding on to our breath, either in anticipation of the next turn of events or simply just hoping our putting the littlest or maximum effort was enough to sustain our goals and aspirations.

But for how long?

For how long do we get to live our lives running against time, pursuing goals, promotion at work, acknowledgement from friends, family, colleagues and superiors at work.

For how long?

Essentially, the train of thought that led me to this was the reality that my mind was burdened by too much than I could grasp when asked to tell it.

What is blocking my happiness?

Of course, I'm happy... but I can't peacefully rest at night or manage my day without dwelling on negative thoughts. There are times I say to myself that I don't want to ask for the obvious; I deserve it to be given to me. Yes, I work hard to attain all the stability I can in life, and it's achieved... but I'm not so stable in my emotions. Sometimes overthinking causes a rise in your emotions because you want reality to be so clear and different, but it's not. Taking things for what they are and not what you want them to be, puts a lot of things to rest and helps to alleviate stress. For example, I was never on social media until November 2022 and only once in college. This was something that I never wanted to do because I have been scorned so many times that everything to me is triggering and causes me to overthink. Overthinking is one of my strengths and weaknesses. It causes me to be prepared for tough situations, but then again, it causes me not to give grace where grace is needed sometimes.

Some of what I need from my life is what my dad used to give me, but which, at that time, I often didn't want. Those small talks, the sympathy, how he was always treating me as if I was still "loved." He lets me know I'm loved verbally and incessantly reminds me of what I could achieve. He was my biggest fan. I don't have this anymore.

I feel lost, I don't know who's on my side, who's rooting for me. Everyone has their own issues and personal struggles, yet I'm the only one voicing them. I hate doing so, for it appears as though I'm complaining. How do you talk to those closest to you about life without guarding up? How, what's the purpose, and who cares?

That was me. Maybe it's still me to certain extents.

While these were manifestations of some of my fears of the unknown, and the fact that my protective mechanisms are often up, they also showed that I needed to recalibrate myself if I really wanted to live fully. I needed to stop being so harsh on myself; stop denying myself the joy of little wins because I've set too many high standards for myself; to recognize and embrace the reality that good and bad times, successes and failures, wins and losses are like yin and yang. They go hand in hand. I needed to accept myself for what I am; everyone around me for what they are; and life for all that it would offer at every turn. Thus, acceptance became yet another important phase in who I am today.

Acceptance in human psychology is a person's assent to the reality of a situation, recognizing a process or condition (often a negative or uncomfortable situation) without attempting to change it or protest it. This happens in cognizance with the fact that we all know that sometimes change is necessary. Any change requires some amount of effort and discipline on our part. The concept is close in meaning to acquiescence, derived from the Latin *acquiēscere* (to find rest in).

Self-Acceptance

Self-acceptance is defined as "an individual's acceptance of all of his/her attributes, positive or negative" It includes body acceptance, self-protection from negative criticism, and believing in one's capacities.

Self-acceptance is being satisfied with one's current self. Consider it an acknowledged agreement with oneself to appreciate, validate, and support oneself as it is, despite one's deficiencies and negative past behavior. People have trouble accepting themselves because of guilt, trauma, or a perceived lack of motivation. Some people have the misconception that if one is happy with themselves, it always means that one would not have to change anything about who they are. However, we do not have to be unhappy with ourselves and can actively change things we don't like. Self-acceptance is a form of growth mechanism in individuals whereby there's this inward assessment of one's values, relationships, goals, intents, and life generally.

This form of acceptance entails unconditionally valuing all parts of who you are. That means you acknowledge all of yourself—both the good and the things that need improvement. The process of self-acceptance starts with acknowledging judgments against yourself and softening those judgments, acknowledging standards you have and softening them so that every part of yourself and the achievements you'd record can be valued. So that every step of the way, you assess yourself fairly from an in-motion or "work in progress" perspective based on knowledge.

Many people have low self-acceptance. There can be many reasons for this, but one widely accepted theory is that because we develop our self-esteem partly from others appreciating us, people with low self-acceptance may have had parents who lacked empathy during their childhood. Consequently, in their adult lives, they may need much stronger affirmation from others than most people do. In other words, ordinary levels of approval do not "move the needle" on their self-esteem.

A major symptom of not accepting yourself is made manifest when we are found criticizing and judging ourselves harshly when involved in all manners of physical, mental, and emotional health issues. It's important to know the symptoms that show you don't love and accept yourself so that you can fix them as soon as possible. Developing a victim mentality which involves believing what other people say about you or seeking approval is another way in which lack of self-acceptance is manifested. At the end of the day, you serve someone else's agenda, not your own.

Failure to accept yourself will eventually lead to low self-confidence because you won't trust yourself. Soon you'll start pitying and hating yourself and this will prevent your growth and development. Lack of self-acceptance leads to inactivity because you'll lack the ability to inspire and motivate yourself to do the things that are good for you such as sleeping properly, eating nutritious foods, and exercising regularly.

Some people with low self-acceptance try to bolster it by accomplishing great things. But this only helps your self-esteem for a while. That's because achievement is a poor substitute for intimacy. In addition, these people are often under the impression that "taking it" when suffering is the main reflection of their value. It's hard for them to believe in genuine caring, and when it does come their way, they are suspicious of it.

Of course, self-acceptance (or lack thereof) does not exist in a vacuum — it has profound effects on your physical and psychological health because accepting yourself means no longer rejecting yourself. Being rejected is bad for your health. Protracted feelings of isolation, loneliness, and rejection tend to coincide with deteriorations in physical health, which can be derived from a lack of eating or exercise. They don't sleep well, their immune systems sputter, and they even tend to die sooner than people who are surrounded by others who care about them. We think if we punish ourselves enough, we'll change. Accepting ourselves unconditionally is difficult because we must give up the fantasy that if we punish ourselves enough with negative thoughts, we'll change, but instead, we make ourselves more anxious. The frightened little child inside of us doesn't respond favorably to such a mean dictator. Instead, we need to find ways to accept the anxious part of ourselves, to hold that part by the hand and gently say, "You are okay."

Additionally, committing yourself to shift your focus from judgment and blame to tolerance and compassion is important. For that reason, it is worth understanding what these effects are and what you can do about them.

How to Accept Oneself

It is a known fact that learning to be OK with all the pieces of oneself can be hard. Most of the time, while there are always ways to improve and better ourselves, in the end, we are who we are. Some of us tend to be critical of ourselves. After all, who doesn't have good qualities they're proud of and flaws they could do without? And we each experience success or failure at different times in our lives.

From the moment we're born, how we fit into the world is determined and highly influenced by our caregivers or parents. This gives them a lot of power in terms of how we understand and see ourselves. For instance, if your parent encouraged, loved, and accepted you, your self-acceptance will often be much different from a child who experienced the opposite. When we start school, we're measured by how well we perform on tests and in class, as well as how we assimilate with our peers. All this can contribute to self-worth and acceptance.

As we get older, life circumstances, relationships, and how we're treated by others can influence how we take care of ourselves mentally. Even though you may not care what others think, you still take it in and process it accordingly. This is very harmful mentally to many people. It causes panic attacks and lack of sleep. The perception of yourself is something that many individuals often take for granted.

> ***Understanding that you are unique and that you are your own superhero is essential.***

It can be hard for many of us to accept ourselves if the reality of concepts such as diversity, equity, and inclusion is low where we live. It could also rear its head out if the Impostor Phenomenon has been at play in your life. By Impostor Phenomenon, I mean a situation where one continually doubts their abilities and feels like a fraud. We readily accept ourselves. So, it's a two-way thing that disproportionately affects high-achieving and goal-driven people, especially those who find it difficult to accept their accomplishments. Also, denying who you are because of low self-esteem is another manifestation of the lack of self-acceptance. These are people who push themselves to think and act like someone else because they feel like they are living a lie because it's not a life of their own making. Denying who you are also involves ignoring your inner voice, which always tells you to be who you are. The result? You'll be stressed, overwhelmed, and angry at yourself. Many also question whether they're deserving of accolades and the big or little wins that come their way.

Also, self-acceptance can be tough for someone who's engaged in harmful behaviors that had consequences; or one whose trauma has made it difficult to embrace the past or live fully in the present. No matter how your self-acceptance was shaped up until this point, there are practical ways to work on accepting yourself, right now, just as you are. If you've had a hard time with self-acceptance in the past, know that there are ways to embrace the present, gain perspective on the past, and love everything in-between. In fact, learning to accept oneself for who they are can bring peace, calm, and some more definition to one's life. With some practice, you can learn the art of self-acceptance too. But it all begins with your state of mind.

If I were to make a list, I'd practically ask to, first, forgive yourself. Afterwards, practice self-compassion, acknowledge and love your abilities while ignoring your inner critic. Next, live in and be aware of the present moment. Then connect with loved ones who appreciate you, and who could help you move on from disappointments. They could also through their honesty help to gain perspective on your limitations. Now, let's put these into practice...

- **Try Self-Forgiveness**

If you have hurt people in the past or acted in ways which when you look back, you are not so proud of, forgiving yourself can feel hard. But it'd be the right thing to do, and doing so does not mean you condone your behavior. Instead, it means you accept what you've done, are ready to take responsibility, and are giving yourself just the right permission to move on.

Forgive yourself and others – You cannot grow and prosper without forgiving yourself and others. Remember, forgiveness is a selfish act. You forgive others so that you can have enough energy to focus on your growth and improvement. Forgive yourself for the mistakes you've made. No one is perfect. Being too hard on yourself or others cannot accelerate your success.

One approach most therapist use to help people practice self-forgiveness incorporates taking responsibility, feeling remorse, restoration of self, and renewal. This process directly improves one's self-esteem, especially as the guilt from passing judgement on oneself is washed away consciously. Although self-esteem differs from self-acceptance, it refers to having confidence in your qualities and abilities. A person with higher self-esteem might feel worthy of good and positive experiences and feel able to handle difficult situations.

In a 2017 study based on data from 201 adolescents, researchers observed that a person's self-esteem was linked to them having fewer symptoms of anxiety, depression, and attention problems. Thus, we could say that self-esteem, and how it translates to the absence of these problems connects it to self-acceptance. As we have come to know, self-acceptance refers to the act of embracing every aspect of yourself —both in strengths and weaknesses.

- **Practice Self-Compassion**

Self-compassion involves giving yourself warmth and understanding during difficult times or when you feel inadequate. It involves practical actions such as talking to yourself like you would to a friend that made a mistake; writing down how you'd like to help yourself; putting your situation into perspective; and engaging in self-care or self-love routines such as meditation, exercise, and healthy eating.

Also, focus on yourself. Instead of looking at other people and working hard to be like them, you should focus on yourself. This means setting your standards and metrics to measure your success. Remember, loving yourself is not selfish. You cannot expect to love others if you don't love yourself. To enhance other peoples' well-being, you need to look after yourself by taking care of your physical and mental health. Don't be afraid to focus and put yourself first.

The lack thereof of this habit usually manifests itself when we find ourselves depending on other people to make us happy. People who don't love themselves cannot be happy with themselves. They'll try micromanaging and controlling other people to feel better about themselves. In short, they are energy vampires. They are also found to be constantly justifying themselves. People who don't love themselves the way they are focus on their good traits and boast so that the people around them can agree with them. They try to get anyone who is listening to believe in what they are saying even if deep down they don't believe in it themselves. Remember, true love is never boastful. Anytime you see a boastful person, you see someone who doubts himself or herself.

The absence of self-love also rears its head in indecisiveness in people who want to seek approval, or they want people to react to their choices. In short, they crave the attention and respect of others. Also, bad things happen to them all the time and they just can't figure it out. They complain and blame others for their misfortunes while forgetting that how they feel about themselves determines what happens to them. They are also always preoccupied with personal problems because their mindset is structured around themselves. They tend to judge themselves harshly because they think everyone is talking about them. They keep going back to the people who dislike them or things that hurt them because they want to prove that they are worthy even if deep inside, they know it's impossible.

Self-love is an important part of self-care and self-compassion. Although society rightly and often tells us how important it is to be selfless in how we take care of others, put loved ones first, and give whatever and whenever we can, we also must learn, at every turn, to do the same for ourselves. Do note that these messages on selflessness themselves aren't wrong. Most people are part of a larger community, and we tend to benefit when we take care of each other. But the problem comes when we prioritize taking care of others over caring for ourselves. This is something I am quite often guilty of doing.

The concept of self-love is simple. It just means that you'd be valuing and caring for your own needs, wants, and desires just as well as you do for others. It isn't about being selfish, rather, it's about making sure you have time to recharge yourself, that you replenish yourself, and have the energy and resources to be there for others. This explains why airlines remind us that it's important to put on your oxygen mask before helping others do the same. This is because if you run out of air, it becomes a lot harder to help anyone, including yourself. If, as a mother, you'd be taking care of everyone and sustaining the home, you'd need to take extra care of yourself such that you don't break down. This is a glaring fact because it becomes even harder to do anything for the people you love when you are not in a good state.

Self-love could also be more radical, such as taking a day off from work to recharge. Here, the goal isn't to be radical in any way, rather, it's to place more importance on oneself. The goal of self-love is usually to love yourself at least as well as you love others. Some major health benefits of practicing self-love include sleeping better, improving eating habits; helping with stress management; and making exercise a consideration.

Do note that although the concept of self-love and self-acceptance are related, they are not the same. While self-love refers to how valuable or worthwhile you see yourself, self-acceptance is a global affirmation of self. Self-acceptance is all about embracing our positive and negative facets. This means that self-acceptance is unconditional. Recognizing and accepting your limitations or weaknesses should not interfere with your ability to accept yourself fully.

To love yourself, you need to explore what parts of yourself you are unwilling to accept. Loving yourself is all about accepting yourself 100%. This is only possible when you stop judging yourself. Our self-esteem likewise rises the moment we stop being so hard on ourselves. Also, despite the many benefits of self-love, this habit receives less attention and practice from people by the day. When you do practice self-love and self-compassion, it can help make you more resilient in times of adversity.

How then do you love yourself?

- **First, escape!**

It's not uncommon to feel drained when you're constantly working to meet the needs of others — especially when you're a mother of four kids like me. And when there are others, kids, and my husband right here, it can be difficult to find some time for self-love. But this is even more reason why taking breaks from those who rely on you most can be so beneficial. Anytime you feel drained, tired, or hating yourself, you are turning your thoughts and emotions against yourself. And this will make your life difficult and that of your loved ones. When we say taking a break, it could be a night at a local hotel (just you) to watch a movie, sleep in, and eat uninterrupted. Perhaps one of the most important forms of self-care, allowing yourself to get the sleep you need, can help you feel your best. Or it could be lunch by yourself with a good book and no one requesting anything of you. These, especially the latter, are some of the best chances at an escape I could get until the kids are much older.

- **Second, I find ways to include spending time in open spaces with nature and my loved ones**

Fresh air and greenery are something I find quite therapeutic. So, I always find ways to include taking the kids out to the park in my weekly schedule. The outdoor adventures and experiences with the people we love can often put a smile on our faces. Yours could include planning a hike with a romantic partner, a bike ride with your kids, a picnic in the community park, or leaning into my childhood experience visiting Disneyland with family.

- **Third, adopting a hobby**

In addition to this is the idea that you could fill your home with things that make you smile. Since the home should be your safe place and sanctuary, consider filling yours with what brings you joy, whether it's live plants, pictures of happy memories, or an art piece you love to look at. These such things could be taken up as projects. It could be volunteering, cultivating a home garden, or decorating.

     Also, I've learned to give myself permission to say 'No.' You can't be everything to everyone, and it's hard to give your best if you're constantly trying to do it all. When you practice saying "no," it allows you to take on what you can handle. If you're not in the habit of telling people "No," like I was, it can initially feel challenging and even anxiety-inducing. With time, you'll get to accept the peace that comes from putting a limit to things you'd let into your space. Still, if you need to say "yes" to someone, you can say it and put limits or boundaries in place. For example, you could say, "Yes, you can come over at 1 p.m., but I'll need you to leave at 3 p.m." You're allowed to draw your own personal lines and stick to them. You don't owe people explanations or the chance to negotiate.

- **Exercise!**

Research has found countless benefits (both mental and physical) to daily exercise. It's not necessary to push yourself too hard, and more isn't always better — a 30-minute walk can be a great way to get your body moving and enjoy the benefits exercise provides. It's common to feel that the motivation to exercise just isn't there, even if you initially wanted to. However, even if keeping fit isn't the goal, the locomotion, and activity that comes with exercises make it easier to relax, sleep better, and even improve one's self esteem. Complementing this is meditation. Meditating helps to improve one's mental health in the long term. It is also another form of exercise that may not be physical but psychological. The easiest way to begin is to find a comfortable and quiet place to sit for 10 minutes. Close your eyes and focus your attention on your breath, heartbeat, and the positive goals you have for the day.

Subtle reminders of your worth could be all the love you can also get. We've all caught ourselves in negative self-talk from time to time, but what if you made a concerted effort to lift yourself up? If you need reminders to do so, you can leave notes around the house that point out what you love best about yourself.

• **Lean into Mindfulness**
While we often cannot control life's circumstances, waking up each day and trying to live more mindfully is possible. For instance, I always try to create a purpose for the following day each night. Something as simple as setting a time to wake up and going on a walk before you work can give you direction. If you want to tackle a bigger purpose like finding your dream job, you might try adding in job searching or updating your resume to the day.

• **Applaud Your Abilities**
Maybe you make a great apple pie or are the person your friends turn to for a listening ear. Or perhaps you're a hard worker or have a green thumb. Whatever your strengths are — no matter how small or big— you could write them down to applaud yourself. You can read the list aloud whenever you're slow to see what's praiseworthy about yourself.

Complementing this is the need to focus on your progress. Most of the time, we get so engrossed in failures and watch certain ideologies we've held so dear fail. Forget about the ideal. Perfection will not take you to the next level. When you focus on your progress, you'll eventually become successful. Keep in mind that there will always be room for improvement no matter how well you do something.

- **Ignore Your Inner Critic**

It's easy to be your own worst critic and listen to your negative thoughts. It's also easy to subject so many aspects of our individual lives to expectations and standards. When this is the case, if our wins do not meet up to those standards, we tend to consider them as losses. That way, we become our own worst critic. But when you feel self-criticism coming on, you can try to put it on hold, take a step back, and think about what you would tell a friend who was thinking that about themselves. Ultimately, it'd be something along the line of, "Consider this as a step in the right direction, or it's a win regardless of how small."

While ignoring this inner criticism that we impose on ourselves, we should also confront our fears. Devastating things happen to all of us. We all have baggage that prevents us from trying something new and hurting ourselves. The fear of failure holds us back from realizing our potential. Most people are afraid of the unfamiliar and they find themselves stuck in their comfort zones. It's important to take baby steps to avoid freaking yourself out when making changes and adjustments. Start by creating a list of the things you've been afraid to do. It could be networking at a key event or asking your boss for a raise. Start with something small and face it. Figure out why you fear doing it. A big victory is made up of many small victories. This was tackled extensively in the preceding chapter on the fear of the unknown.

In line with this is the fact that we should all mourn but be able to move on from unsatisfied aspirations. When your hopes and dreams aren't met, it's easy to feel disappointed. While allowing yourself to feel disappointed is healthy, moving on when you're ready can also help. You could try memorializing the effort to strive for that vision in life and closing that chapter mentally in favor of a new goal.

- **Cultivate Your Inner Circle**

To fully accept ourselves and be accepted in return, we should also surround ourselves with positive people. It is said that one's company will determine how high you go in your personal and professional life. Surrounding yourself with negative people cannot make you a positive person. Feeding your mind in the world's worst minds won't lighten up your inner world. Therefore, it's important to choose your company carefully. Associate with positive people who will help you confront your fears. Apart from that, focus on the positive aspects of life. Remember, your mind is like a piece of land. When you take your time to cultivate it, it will bring forth sweet fruits. If you don't cultivate it, weeds will grow naturally. And once they take over, eliminating them will be very difficult.

There's nothing like family and friends that you can trust and share your deepest thoughts, concerns, and funny stories with. Surrounding yourself with people who welcome you for who you are is a great way to feel accepted. While on most occasions, it can be tiring having to be the caregiver for one's family and close friends, especially when one expects the same amount of energy back, they're just about the only one to go to when the need to unwind or rebuild oneself arises. Also, like-minded people can be found in every community. In my own case, the Academy I grew up with serves as ample provision for the many online support groups or forums that exist today.

- **Realize Acceptance is Not Settling**

Accepting your flaws and failures does not mean you're settling for less. In fact, knowing your limitations can go a long way for your mental well-being as long as you don't give up. When you fall, you must get up and keep on keeping on. When we fail, we learn more about ourselves than when we succeed. Figure out what needs to be done and just do it. At the end of the day, celebrate having the courage to go after what you want. For instance, instead of focusing on how impatient you are with children, embrace how well you connect with older individuals by visiting your grandparents often or volunteering at a nursing home. In the same way that it gets tiring trying not to expect from people the same level of commitment that I give does not mean that I have to stop helping or caring. When COVID occurred, there were a lot of changes the world encountered. I still had the same goals and was not willing to settle. I gave birth to two children during covid, one at the beginning and one at the end. I saw clients again face to face, got out of the house, and serviced those in need. Mental health is essential, and knowing your worth and what you can do to make a difference in someone's life was what helped me to grow and become stronger and of course, more tired lol.

Also, don't take things personally. If someone or something offends you, don't take it personally. Don't assume that you know what people mean. Stop defending or justifying yourself. When you stop taking things personally, you'll realize that people are doing their best to make things work. Plus, they might be having a bad day, which is not your fault.

- **Validate Yourself**

Everyone needs validation —to feel accepted and understood. It's normal to want validation from others—your parents, spouse, boss, friends—but some of us seek external validation to an unhealthy level. We rely on others to make us feel good. We doubt our abilities if we're not explicitly told we're doing well. We obsessively check our social media posts looking for approval. And we question our worth if others don't value us.

However, we can't always get validation from others. Therefore, it's important to know how to validate ourselves. It feels good to be praised, to have your feelings affirmed, to be told you did a good job, and to be appreciated. Relying on external validation can make us anxious or depressed. A lack of self-confidence may cause us to make more errors and have trouble concentrating. And disapproval and criticism are especially painful because we put so much stock into other people's opinions.

We can't rely on others to make us feel good. When we do, we allow others to dictate our worth. And we don't trust our own thoughts, feelings, and judgments; we assume others know more than we do, and their opinions matter more. We become needy and ask for validation in ways that turn others off – in ways that scream my self-esteem is lacking and I need you to tell me I'm okay.

Instead, you can learn how to validate yourself. External validation should be in addition to self-validation, not in place of it.

Self-validation is a skill that takes practice. It includes encouraging yourself, acknowledging your strengths, successes, progress, and effort, noticing and accepting your feelings, prioritizing your needs, treating yourself with kindness, saying nice things to yourself, and accepting your limitations, flaws, and mistakes. It won't be easy at first. To begin, try to do or say at least one self-validating thing per day (see ideas below). Then, after you've got that down, strive for two, and so on. With practice, it will become second nature to validate yourself. And as you get better at validating yourself, you'll seek less external validation and have less tolerance for people invalidating you, too. Self-criticism, comparing yourself to others, minimizing or denying your needs and feelings, perfectionism, and judging yourself harshly are not validating.

Importance of Self-Acceptance

Acceptance means that we can look into the face of the present and say, "I see you, and I acknowledge you are here."

We usually set standards that are too high for ourselves because society expects us to be perfect. We tend to forget that everyone has flaws, including those we perceive as perfect. Self-love and self-acceptance are critical aspects of health and happiness. These are the attributes that shape our physical, mental, and emotional health in real and concrete ways. When we refuse to accept ourselves, we cut ourselves from the energy that sustains life. This process happens gradually as we are disconnected from the life force. And this leads to serious health issues.

In essence, self-acceptance is synonymous with recognizing that we need to make our own choices as well as deal with their consequences. Learning to make your own choices is one area that we all must be able to do. Making your own choices can look like something simple, like deciding where to go for dinner, or something more complex, like deciding to say no to the offer to come to work on a Saturday when you already plan to spend the whole day sleeping in and rejuvenating. Taking control of your situation is important. You must learn to make your own choices and not be influenced by those around you. You have your best interest in mind, especially since not everyone else does.

Self-acceptance means that you understand who you truly are and where your strengths and weaknesses lie. You know what you want. This will allow you to be comfortable with your place in the world and be honest with yourself. This is very important for several reasons. The first is that if you know who you are, you can be more confident about that person. You can also be more authentic rather than trying to be something else. This should make you feel comfortable in your own skin and less stressed.

In line with the above is the materialization of responsibility. If you make a decision, it's best to always prepare for the consequences. "For every action, there is a reaction," and that's a valid argument. So, when you make a mistake, taking responsibility for your actions is important. This is especially true if you hurt someone's feelings with your words, action, or inaction. If you have come to terms with what made you do what you did, you're able to truly apologize and say, "I messed up. That's on me." If you can't accept and take responsibility for your actions, you aren't as self-reliant, nor have you accepted yourself as well as the implication of your action, as much as you think.

When we don't accept ourselves the way we are, we are, in essence, wearing ourselves out internally. And when we fight against ourselves, guess who loses? It's important to accept the fact that we all have flaws. Everyone makes mistakes. Making mistakes is not a bad thing that you should avoid completely. It's one of the best ways to learn and grow. Accepting our strengths and weaknesses and reconciling the conflicting parts in our inner world is critical to our health and happiness. Plus, you cannot achieve anything substantial in the outer world without fixing your inner world.

Self-acceptance has also allowed me to personalize and own my recovery from the bottom of my problems. Acceptance encourages us to move away from the past or how much it hurts us and move into the future. Your future is yours and yours alone, so own your recovery. Allow yourself to make decisions that will benefit your short- and long-term recovery. You get to choose how to move forward, so make sure you are thinking through your decisions. Healthy self-acceptance is all about balance, so don't make a rash decision that's fueled by emotions. Think your decisions through with a level head. The decision to write this book, to share my story was one of the many steps required of me to recover fully from my own pains.

Honesty! This simply means that we want to stick to the facts in what would be the fairest and most straightforward ways possible. If you accept yourself, you can decide more honestly about what you can do to use your strengths to their best effect. Which career would best suit you? What lifestyle do you long for? Or how best would you want to raise your kids, and in what ideal environment would you prefer. With self-acceptance you can respect your answers as directly derived from an institution of facts rather than trying to be what others expect of you. With self-acceptance comes choice and you can make it honestly, too. If you don't accept things for what they are, you may just never know peace. This isn't an excuse to turn away from doing the right thing. No, you should never accept cruelty or hate or injustice. However, there are things you must accept or else you'll live a life of bitterness and dissatisfaction. This includes such things as the inevitability of aging and death. No one escapes these so it's pointless to go against them. There is a certain beauty in the quality of life. Once you come to terms with that, you value every day as the gift it is.

Acceptance also reduces self-criticism. This is a form of negative self-talk. This self-talk is often highly critical and can hold a person back in their efforts. Self-acceptance, however, involves accepting some things we may not like about ourselves, and by doing so, it provides a basis for positive change. In the above definitions of self-acceptance, it is one with completely independent thinking that does not rely on anybody else's opinion. If you can accept yourself honestly, you may be able to ignore what others believe about you. Criticism from others is often a major cause of low self-esteem. Thus, being grounded in one's weaknesses and strengths means no criticism can be taken seriously. It'd instead be a new song we are already too familiar with. Freeing ourselves from self-criticism, you can then begin to face the challenges in your life and overcome them. Imagine being at ease with people, being able to speak in public, and feeling good about yourself.

The importance of self-acceptance can also be seen because it reduces the pressure and stress you might be giving yourself. Perfectionism is often a problem that honest acceptance can moderate. In the relationship between parents and their children, for example, the experience of antagonism of the latter to the former is usually based on the criticism of how the child is not living according to the parents' standards or abandoned goal which the child is supposed to pick up as a legacy to last a lifetime. Being too hard and trying to be perfect causes these issues to arise.

Accepting One's Partner

Acceptance in marriage or any form of partnership is a necessity for growth. It also makes it easier to appreciate the good things about your partner and your relationship, leading you towards greater intimacy and care for each other. It basically helps to keep your relationship healthy. When you and your partner feel accepted, you're more willing to listen to and understand each other's perspectives and suggestions.

Acceptance is about valuing your partner's differences. It's about being flexible, tolerant, and open-minded. It's also about knowing how to compromise, understanding that we all make mistakes, and being ready to forgive. I've come to know that acceptance doesn't mean always agreeing with your partner. It's OK to agree to disagree. But it does mean believing that your partner is trying to do the right thing.

All of this means acceptance creates a healthier, happier, and more positive environment for the whole family. This can strengthen your relationship and make it easier for you and your partner to work as a parenting team. Raising children in this kind of environment is good for their development and can help them thrive. I am indeed grateful for Jason and how much he's helped to build our amazing family.

We have continued to strengthen this beautiful thing that we have through spending so much time on shared interests, such as starting our own business. On so many occasions, he'd let me sleep in while looking after the children. That, right there, is a golden ticket to manifest or show love and appreciation to one's partner. Often, we reminisce on how and when we first met, the activities we did together, things we liked, and how we'd always do those things again and talk about the happy times we've had together.

Summarily, acceptance has become a very important reality in my life. When I stopped living in the problem and began living in the answer, the problem went away. And till today, acceptance is the answer to all my problems. When I am disturbed, it is because I find some person, place, thing, or situation –some fact of my life– unacceptable to me. I can find no serenity until I accept that person, place, thing, or situation as being exactly the way it is supposed to be at the moment.

CHAPTER SUMMARY

I know my purpose in life. It involves helping those who can't help themselves... but I'm in that same bracket. I may be physically and mentally able to sustain life and its tribulations, but I can't ascertain who will observe me and ensure I'm ok. I may not always be able to say how I feel because I can't put it into words. I'm so guarded yet so open to comfort. I have accepted certain realities around me.

Of course, balancing life and cherishing moments is key. Some may keep wanting what a person can't give and don't have in them to do. Accepting that everyone isn't going to perform as you do is another reality, and accepting the struggles that come along with this is a rather big challenge. I guess it's true to expect the unexpected. Don't expect anything in return, regardless of whether it's a physical or mental gain.

We could surmise that we all must have, at some point or the other, missed the first and most crucial step of all. That first step requires that we unconditionally value all parts of who we are. With this, we become poised to accept our reality. We acknowledge any role we may have played, good or bad, in getting where we are. We ask ourselves questions about our respective situations to help work toward solutions towards a goal. We are able to reconcile the conflicting parts of our inner world as is critical to achieve anything substantial in the outer world, to achieve happiness and live fully.

A trademark of people who rank high on the acceptance board include:

- A positive self-attitude
- Acknowledgment and acceptance of all aspects of themselves (including the good and bad),
- Not being self-critical or confused about their identity
- Do not wish they were any different from who they already are

Without accepting ourselves and the world of people and events around us, we are left to be riddled by:

- The failure to accept oneself and the eventual low self-confidence
- Accomplishing great things as only a temporary boost to self-esteem for a while
- Criticizing and judging ourselves harshly when involved in all manners of physical, mental, and emotional health issues
- The dependence of our self-esteem, in part, from others appreciating us

To Accept oneself and life generally, it is recommended to:

- Attempt self-forgiveness
- Practice self-compassion and self-love through escape, including visits to open natural spaces, adopting a pet or mini project, exercising, saying 'no' to people so they don't intrude on one's peace, and placing around subtle reminders
- Lean into mindfulness
- Applaud one's abilities and little wins
- Ignore the inner critic
- Cultivate your inner circle
- Realize that acceptance is not settling for less
- Validate yourself

Essentially, with acceptance and the recognition that everyone at every phase of the way, doing their best is in the pursuit of something beyond your personal self. It becomes imperative to set the same standards in your personal life as you do professionally, to put in the same time and energy into maintaining a bond with your mate as you do with your staff to ensure optimum performance and results.

While facing reality isn't the easiest thing to do, accepting your current situation can make you happier in the present and lead to a better future. Understanding, accepting, and working with reality is both practical and purposeful. Acknowledging your reality will help you choose your dreams wisely and then help you achieve them.

Also, acceptance is necessary for the healing process. To practice acceptance, you must acknowledge all the uncomfortable parts of yourself: your emotions, your thoughts, your past, and your fears, just as well. Practicing acceptance is kind of like taking care of the dirty clothes hamper in your room. You fill it with your clothes throughout the weeks, and it piles up. Work is tiring, cleaning the rest of the house is enough of a chore, and life keeps getting in the way. You know that the hamper is there, but you've been ignoring the real mess of clothes inside. After enough time passes, you may even forget that you own some of the clothes at the bottom of that basket. Finally, the day comes when you acknowledge that the corner of your room is a real mess, you're short on clothes, and it's time to do laundry. As you take out each piece to wash and hang them, you're acknowledging the separate pieces of the mess and accepting the situation and the tasks necessary to clean up—much like when you take your personal inventory and accept that you are imperfect, that there are parts of yourself and your psyche that you must work to heal.

EPILOGUE

I'll toast to this book becoming one of many surreal life examples of what we experience daily that we are afraid to share with others. I live by, and always will, to "treat others as we want to be treated."

This quote describes me as a whole. Regardless of what others have done to me or their wavering intentions, I always go above and beyond to ensure that those I love are cared for and that they know that I love them. More often than not, I cannot help but reflect on the processes that led to this moment.

Does the accumulation of knowledge and degrees translate to definite answers as to who I am?

Of course, having run through my personal life in its brevity, the walk, leaps, and quick steps of growth through the many distractions, self-doubts, and fears of the unknown have only led me to accept myself to one place. Here. Right where I get to understand and unravel every shade of who I am. Through this phase, I could categorically say that the person that I am at the end of the day, at the end of this book, is a businesswoman, a wife, a mother of four, a sister, an aunt, a friend, and many more roles. I am one and all of these things with a story attached to each.

I'm always trying to figure out who I am. Maybe that'll never end. Maybe I will have a glimpse of who I am and be able to relate my experiences to new adventures. I want to learn from my experiences and turn them into something fulfilling. Take your losses as lessons and continue to grow. Don't worry about what others think of you, and continue to move forward, especially since this is a story yet to be told in its entirety. It's one in transition.

In the next phase, as would be heralded by this assembly of my experiences and knowledge on different issues peculiar to women and to everyone generally, I intend to have and improve on this mount of fulfilling moments with family.

Oftentimes, however, I live in my own mind wondering what I can do for people to make sure that they don't hurt me instead of figuring out how I will not hurt myself and how I will stay true to what I want to do. So, I've learned along the way that I am my own best image, so it's up to me to make the decision; to make myself feel better. I also often reiterate that until I heal from within, then I will enjoy life.

At other times, I simply just continue to mope and pout that I won't get where I want to get in life. I mean, with the trials and tribulations I've been through, using them as needed as motivation to move forward and help other people around me could be tough. Through these periods, it helped that I found a sense of self in motherhood. A sense of self refers to your perception of the collection of characteristics that define you. It is so easy to lose yourself in the guise of motherhood that only by pursuing your dreams can you help be able to preserve a sense of self. You feel fulfilled when you pursue your dreams when you do something for yourself.

Although it might take several years, the guise of motherhood would surely end. By that, I mean that there will be a time when we will have raised kids big enough to stand on their own two feet. How will your life look when that time comes? Will you have something to do when your kids are out of the house? Are you going to be happy then with the decision to pursue your dreams now or to put your dreams on hold now until when you become an empty nester?

I'm in a field where I come across a lot of different situations, but a lot of which I can relate to. That may be why this has been my current and only profession. I can relate to a lot of situations. I'm adaptable. I'm able to understand. Mostly, I would like to make people aware of the need to "trust the process." I do not know about you, but I know what it feels like to attend a Zoom meeting with my notepad next to my chopping board while I am preparing dinner for my family. Watching and creating synergy between family life and career pursuit is usually fun and eventful. In the end, we must do whatever we can to live our purpose.

Erica Nicole

To pursue our mommy dreams, however, I have discovered that I'd require both internal and external work. Doing the internal work would encompass self-care and its branches – including self-acceptance and self-compassion. Externally, a whole lot of help is needed. Therefore, I'd advise you not to be afraid to ask for help. Find a number two and a number three person. These people, for me are my husband and close relatives combined. In the workplace, just as at home, you need to build tremendous support. With the increased mobility of society, not all families have extended family support. If you don't have family available in town, seek out the help of co-workers, friends, and neighbors. Line up a couple of co-workers that your children can call to deal with their questions or situations when you are unavailable.

Another major lesson that was the hardest pill to swallow was the realization that I was not going to have it all at the same time. It is laughable at this moment as I'm writing this because if you are anything like me, you want a clean house, laundry washed, ironed, and packed, home-cooked meals every day, time with your loved ones, and time for self-care. Do not get me wrong, you can want these, but wanting them at the same time is not realistic. This was one of the reasons for some of the major breakdowns that I experienced along the way. The reality is that our dreams tend to take the knock when we chase perfection. Therefore, we often need to be sensitive to the season of life that we are in and give ourselves some grace. Moreover, it is advisable to reflect on your days and your weeks to see what worked and what didn't. Life is lived in seasons... If something doesn't work the first time, there's always another opportunity to try again. If you are focused and believe in yourself, then it is only right to allow yourself and trust yourself enough to be happy and fulfilled. Cut things off that are holding you back.

Through my 34 years, I've put these realities here. For my distractions and the effect that they have on me as a person, I acknowledge that they alter the foundation and pathway to my numerous and specific goals, aspirations, and trust. While positive thinking may determine one's perception of things around them and, at the same time, redirect the energy core, the absence of traction alters that sense of direction. Excuses are often presented as capable replacements, thus creating a routine around the affected dynamics. To rid of these internal and external distractions, it is recommended to master your internal triggers, convert your values and goals into practical variables or steps/plans, talk to and be around like-minds, manage your external triggers, and commit to the goal.

Fear, on the other hand, conquers all in most measures. Although it is a cognitive ability innate to every one of us, it is normal to occasionally worry, have negative thoughts, or experience a sense of fear or dread about future events, obligations, or situations. But when these supposed reactions to thoughts, situations, and things yet to happen shape how we act or influence the ways we do not act, there is a problem. Some people fear what may or may not happen. This is a huge struggle I have daily. Every day I struggle with ensuring I am ready for the unknown and putting forth my best efforts. I tend to live in fear and often hold myself back from crossing off things from my to-do list. Why? As individuals, fear helps shape us and mold us to be stronger than the day before. It helps to provide us with the tools we need to grow and to learn. This is called life. Although this is one thing I struggle with, I continue tackling life with a shield regardless of what I encounter on a daily basis.

Fear is a distraction that ruins success, ruins further progression in life, and ruins existence. Being more present as opposed to living with our 'heads in the cloud,' avoiding avoidance, practicing mindfulness, self-care, and better self-esteem are some recommended measures to rid oneself of fears of the unknown. By holding fear as a distraction, oftentimes, as individuals, we end up not reaching "short" term goals, and they become " long" term goals. Knowing who you are as an individual adds to your overall self-worth and happiness. This helps you to live in your truth and to experience life on a different level.

Further, in my pursuit of happiness, fulfillment, and a sense of self, acceptance became the go-to. It's important to remember that acceptance is not synonymous with tolerance. Acceptance is not the reluctant sigh at the end of a stressful day, nor the disgruntled statement, "It is what it is," or "This is just who I am," No, acceptance is total mindfulness grounded in reality. Never sell yourself short. You may always be busy, but as long as you're busy helping others and loving what you're doing, you can't go wrong.

My future goal is to enjoy the moments in life. To not overthink and to go with what makes me "whole,"; to not settle or hold back, and to give as much more of me than before.

Erica Nicole

To today's young people, I would say enjoy the moments in life and take advantage of your resources. Explore outside your comfort zone and gain knowledge in all areas to become well-rounded enough to adapt to this ever-changing world. That is one thing I intend to pass on to my kids. I've recognized that the very first example your children have of motherhood or whatever they'd aim to become is you. I sure have noticed at least once how my children mimic something I did or how I said something. It is no lie that how they grow will be linked to how you parent. Encouraging them to pursue their dreams is not enough, I must show them that it can be done. This is the essence of a woman's journey.

www.ingramcontent.com/pod-product-compliance
Lightning Source LLC
Chambersburg PA
CBHW061731070526
44583CB00024B/3089